MEN-AT-ARMS SERI[ES]

EDITOR: MARTIN WINDR[OW]

Rome's Enemies (3):
Parthians and Sassanid Persians

Text by PETER WILCOX

Colour plates by ANGUS McBRIDE

OSPREY PUBLISHING LONDON

Published in 1986 by
Osprey Publishing Ltd
Member company of the George Philip Group
12–14 Long Acre, London WC2E 9LP
© Copyright 1986 Osprey Publishing Ltd

British Library Cataloguing in Publication Data

Wilcox, Peter
    Rome's enemies.—(Men-at-arms series; 175)
    3: Parthians and Sassanid Persians
    1. Arms and armor, Ancient—History
    I. Title   II. Series
    623.4'09   U805

    ISBN 0-85045-688-6

Filmset in Great Britain
Printed through Bookbuilders Ltd, Hong Kong

Artist's Note

Readers may care to note that the original paintings
from which the colour plates in this book were
prepared are available for private sale. All
reproduction copyright whatsoever is retained by the
publisher. All enquiries should be addressed to:
    Scorpio Gallery
    50 High Street,
    Battle,
    Sussex TN33 0EN
The publishers regret that they can enter into no
correspondence upon this matter.

Rome's Enemies (3): Parthians and Sassanid Persians

Chronology

250 BC	Provinces of Parthia and Greco-Bactria secede from Seleucid Empire.
220 BC	Parthians overrun several eastern provinces of Seleucid Empire.
209 BC	Antiochus III, King of Seleucia, defeats Parthians, halts the Greco-Bactrian expansion.
197 BC	Romans defeat Macedonians at Cynoscephalae, Thessaly.
190 BC	Romans defeat Antiochus III at Magnesia, Lydia.
170–68 BC	Mithridates I leads Parthians to conquest of Elymais, Persia, Media and Bactria.
141 BC	Parthians take control of Mesopotamia from Seleucids.
135 BC	Nomadic Iranian Saka begin raiding eastern provinces of Iran.
95 BC	Parthians regain control of eastern Iran; some Saka remain as subject marchmen of Parthia.
64 BC	Western Asian coast annexed by Rome from Pontus in north to Egypt in south; kingdoms of the interior are made vassals, other states bow to Roman suzerainty.
53 BC	Parthians destroy most of Roman army of the east under Marcus Licinius Crassus, proconsul of Syria, at Carrhae.
52 BC	Armenia and Transcaucasia leave Roman control.
AD **20**	Augustus Caesar regains Armenia and Transcaucasia. Roman standards lost at Carrhae are returned by the Parthians.

Sanatruqu, King of Hatra: a statue showing Parthian court dress of the 2nd century BC. (State Organisation of Antiquities and Heritage, Baghdad)

AD 53	A ten-year war begins between Rome and Parthia over control of Armenia.
AD 63	Roman army of the east increased by two legions, one from Spain, one from Dalmatia.
AD 115	Parthia invaded by Roman army.
AD 117	Roman forces pulled back to Euphrates line by Hadrian.
AD 118–9	Roman advances in Mesopotamia.
AD 226	Parthian monarchy overthrown by Sassanian Persians.
AD 260	Sassanians capture Emperor Valerian and successively reduce Roman fortresses in Mesopotamia.
AD 297	Successful campaigns by Romans in the east; Mesopotamian territories return to Roman occupation.
AD 362	Roman Emperor Julian dies in battle against Sassanians. Many western units of Roman army transferred to the east.
AD 372	Huns (Mongoloid nomads of the Volga) destroy Germanic occupation of western steppes.
AD 410	Northern frontier of Roman Empire caves in; Germanic tribes pour into the western provinces.
AD 440	Kushans (settled Iranian nomads) wiped out by 'White Huns' (Mongoloid nomads of the Altai), who proceed to terrorise eastern Parthia.
AD 484	Sassanian king Peroz killed by White Huns.
AD 552	Turks (non-Iranian white nomads) defeat their overlords the Jwen Jwen (Mongoloid nomads) on Altai plains, Mongolia.
AD 553	Turks break army of White Huns. Sassanians claim the victory, quickly move into White Hunnish territory south of Oxus River. Jwen Jwen and White Hun remnants become the Avars.
AD 600	Sassanian king Chosroes II flees from internal dissension to Byzantium.
AD 601	Chosroes II restored to throne by Byzantine Emperor Maurice. Iberia and much of Armenia ceded to Byzantium.
AD 607	Byzantine forts attacked in Mesopotamia by Sassanian forces; Armenia occupied and Anatolia invaded.
AD 616	Egypt occupied by Sassanians.
AD 623	Byzantines and their Khazar (Turkish nomad) mercenaries march through Lazica and Georgia, attack Persian homelands.
AD 628	Sassanian capital Ctesiphon captured by Byzantines; Chosroes II killed by Sassanian nobles, who sue for peace.
AD 629	Byzantine territories in the east restored.
AD 637	Arabs destroy Sassanian army at Qadisiyya.
AD 642	Imperial Sassanian army defeated at Nihawand, known among Moslems as the 'Victory of Victories'.
AD 649	Sassanian Persia completely overrun by Moslem Arabs.

Introduction

Between 334 and 330 BC the huge Achaemenid Persian Empire tottered to destruction at the hands of the highly professional army of Alexander the Great[1]. Soon after the conquest Alexander set about Hellenising the Medo-Persian aristocracy. His conquests were only half consolidated into a rational organism when, in 323 BC, he died. Within 20 years his Macedonian generals had taken Alexander's empire apart: Cassander was king of Macedonia, Ptolemy of Egypt, Lysimachus of Thrace, Antigonus of Anatolia and Seleucus of Iran. (Collectively these monarchs are known as 'the Successors'.)

A reduced version of the old Achaemenid Imperial territories fell to Seleucus. He and the later 'Seleucids' struggled to regain the lost unity of Alexander's empire. The overwhelming political and military problems of the Seleucids were increased when in 197 BC Rome, disturbed at the growing alliance between the Seleucids and Macedon, despatched two legions to Thessaly in eastern Greece, where they broke the phalanxes of Philip V of Macedonia at Cynoscephalae. When

[1]See MAA 148, *The Army of Alexander the Great*.

the Seleucid king Antiochus III attempted to protect his interests in Ionia and Thrace, the Roman Senate declared war in 192 BC, believing Seleucid interests were a mere beachhead for the invasion of Europe. The army which Antiochus III sent to Greece was speedily worried out again by the Roman army, which in due course crossed to Asia Minor and routed the Seleucid army at Magnesia, Lydia, in 190 BC.

The resulting military weakness and loss of political power by the Seleucids initiated the rise of Parthian dominance in the eastern provinces of Iran. The leading Parthian family belonged to the paramount Scythian clan of the Parni. During their reign the Parthians became a military aristocracy ruling a vast Iranian empire, with influence stretching far beyond its borders. These northern Iranians were never accepted by the settled, southern Iranians, though the payment of homage and reasonable tribute were the only demands made of their subjects by these Arsacid Parthians. The Hellenised petty states were never brought

fully under control, and local rulers seized any opportunity to side with the Seleucids or later Romans. It is not surprising, therefore, that Parthian rulers were apt to look for military help from the Iranian nomad tribes they had left behind on the great plains beyond the Caspian, where links with their kinsmen remained strong.

Chinese military activity and influence among the nomadic tribes of the steppes played a considerable part in the periodic disruption of the north-eastern frontier of Iran throughout the Partho-Sassanian period. Considerable trade was carried out between China and Iran with little interruption, the difficult overland route involving lengthy passages across the high steppes and deserts between northern China and Iran. Chinese embassies were sent to the Parthian Empire, where

Hellenic cuirasses of the 1st century AD. These are depicted being worn by Palmyran gods in high-relief carvings now in the Louvre. They show types of late Greek armours available to the cities of the Near East; one is of lamellar construction, and the other of large overlapping plates. Both are worn with *pteruges* of Roman type.

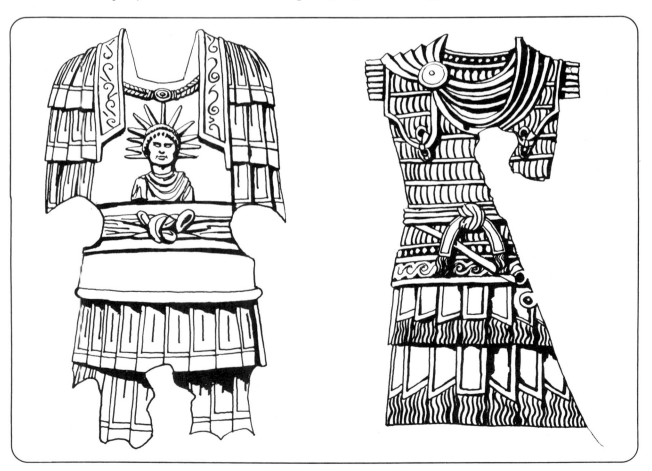

they were able to trade gold and silk for Ferghana horses and other local products. It was from Parthia that knowledge of silk spread to the Greco-Roman world in the 1st century BC, and Parthia was well placed to become the middle-man on the great silk road. The route from China passed along the foothills of the Altyn Tagh-Nan Shan mountains to Lop-Nor, continuing across Chinese Turkestan to Kashgar, skirted the Taklamakan desert, crossed the Pamir high plateau, entered the oases of Ferghana through Merv, and thus into Parthia. (In AD 224 the control of the silk road fell to the Sassanians, and in the 6th century they were able to reach an agreement with other importers which enabled them to create a monopoly, resulting in a steep rise in the silk price on the Roman market, until in AD 552 some eggs of the silk moth, *bombyx mori*, were smuggled into Constantinople in a bamboo cane. This incident, in time, gave the Romans a native silk industry.)

The Parthians

'On horses they go to war, to banquets, to public and private tasks and on them they travel, stay still, do business and chat.' (Justinus, on the Parthians, 2nd century AD)

The Parthians were a Scythian people. From about 700 BC the Scythians proper occupied an area north of the Danube and east of the Carpathians, across the grasslands of east central Europe and southern Russia to the Don. Beyond the Don and stretching to the Chinese hinterland were other mounted Iranian nomads such as Sarmatians, Massagetae and Saka. The whole vast complex was in fact a continuous cultural zone, with a highly developed technology evolved to cope with a difficult environment.

There is little to show that the Scythians were anything but northern Caucasians, very similar to the Celts. Exhaustive examination of the great *kurgans* of the Royal Scyths, which contain skeletal remains of pure Scythians, fits them into a Nordic category. The realistic gold repoussé work on such pieces as the Kul Oba Vase show Scythian warriors in life[1]: their faces are strikingly similar to modern

[1]See MAA 137, *The Scythians 700–300 BC.*

north-west Europeans. The Parthians were typical of Iranians unaltered by admixture with another Caucasoid or Mongoloid group.

The Parthians belonged to the Parni, a branch of the Dahae confederation of Scythian tribes. They were not new arrivals in the Persian arena. In the seventh book of his history Herodotus lists the contingents, weapons and dress of the Persian Imperial forces involved in the invasion of Greece in the 4th century BC during the reign of Xerxes: the Parthians are listed with the Choriasmii under the command of the satrap Artabazus. They were armed with a bow, short sword and spears, no shields were carried. Dress included a tall *bashlyk* cap with long tail and earpieces, close fitting tunic, trousers, ankle boots, and a lidded quiver slung from the waistbelt on the left side. Parthian tribute-bearers appear on the staircase bas-reliefs leading to the Apadana of the palace at Persopolis in Fars built by Darius the Great in the 5th century BC. They are shown in thimble-shaped enclosed hats, long belted coats, long trousers and ankle boots.

The Parthian Army

The feudal system of the Parthians had a Scythian as well as an Achaemenid background, and roughly resembled feudalism as developed in Europe during the 'Dark Ages'. Society was headed by seven powerful clans. This upper stratum supported a petty aristocracy of varied socio-economic status who, together with their retainers, enjoyed status well above the peasants and serfs, who were native Persians. Loyalty was strongest between the great clan leaders and their small vassals. The king, as a member of one of the clans, could usually command complete loyalty from his own clan and its vassals, less from other Parthians.

The crown did not pass from father to son as of right. Worthiness to lead was weighed and opinion expressed by the aristocratic clan leaders in council. While the monarchy was new the great lords were its strength. During most of the Parthian history, however, the nobles were allowed to dominate the monarchy to such a degree that internecine warfare was endemic. Kings were made and unmade, sometimes with outside help from either Rome or the nomads.

The Parthians were a warrior people. Though possessing no regular army they were superb

Drawings of Iranian horsemen. The larger figure—one of the better-known puzzles of ancient military detective-work—is a crude graffito found at Dura Europos, and is of great interest. It depicts a fully-armed *clibanarius* of the 2nd century AD. He wears a conical helmet constructed of metal plates and plumed with streamers; an aventail of mail hangs from the lower edge completely covering the face except for the eyes.

The upper torso is protected with mail, below which are two rows of vertical plates, the top overlapping the lower, from which a skirt of mail is suspended. His limbs are encased in metal rings or hoops. The horse is covered with a trapper of scale construction. What appears to be a mace is carried above the rider's right thigh. The other cavalrymen are equipped in the fashion of light Parthian horse-archers. See Plate C1.

7

Mounted Iranian bowmen. The central figure shows a horse-archer shooting at the gallop; it is taken from a graffito at Dura Europos, and probably depicts the type of horseman found in the lighter of the two great divisions of the Parthian army. The bottom figure is a dynamic little terracotta of the Parthian period now in the Staatliche-Museum, Berlin; he is at the full draw, with three arrows held ready in his bow hand for 'rapid fire'. We are reminded of the way Crassus' troops at Carrhae were peppered with arrows for hours on end by the archers of Surena. The small sketch at top is taken from a silver bowl of the Sassanian period, showing King Chosroes I making a 'Parthian shot' while hunting Argali rams—6th century AD, from the Hermitage Museum, Leningrad.

horsemen and archers, and in time of war the nobility provided heavily armoured knights mounted on weight-carrying chargers. The mass of lesser nobles and their retainers were traditional horse-archers, mounted on tough steppe ponies and armed with the reflex bow. The infantry was composed of good quality hillmen, and of peasants, who were of indifferent military worth.

The Parthian army usually took the field with its heavy assault cavalry protected by fast, light, hit-and-run mounted bowmen. The proportional balance of an army at a given engagement varied widely. Large numbers of *clibanarii* might be accompanied by equal numbers of horse-archers; or relatively few heavy troopers might appear with masses of horse-archers.

Cataphracts or *clibanarii* were heavy enough to break any other type of cavalry which opposed them; they were reasonably immune from hand-propelled missiles and arrows, less so from sling pellets or machine weapons. Their attack would be carried out at an ambling trot in close order, and was often only a feint to cause infantry to regroup into close formation to enable the mounted bowmen to create havoc, thus producing a close order/open order dilemma in the ranks. If the charge was pressed home against infantry who had been subjected to prolonged missile attack, who were suffering from lack of food, water, or rest, or who were already disordered, the chance of success was high. Good, fresh, well-prepared infantry in dense formation were difficult if not impossible to break and could prove disastrously lethal.

Horse-archers were almost impossible to destroy; however, they could be dispersed by good light cavalry, who might in turn be open to eventual counterattack. Enemy cavalry could be attacked while the bowmen's own cataphracts threatened any enemy counterattacking. The effect on heavy infantry was more demoralising than destructive. At Carrhae, it is believed that 20,000 Roman troops out of a force of about 36,000 died at the hands of the Parthians. Whatever the proportion actually killed by horse-archers, the lion's share was credited to them by the Greek historian Plutarch. Concentrated fire directed at a given point of the enemy line could produce an opening for cataphracts to break into.

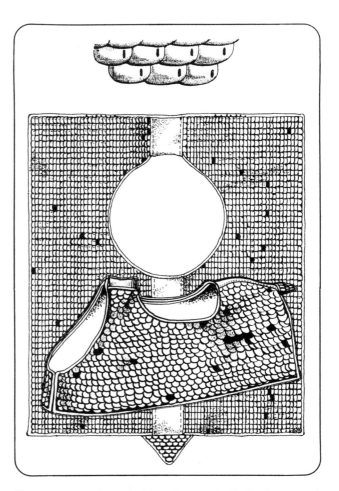

Horse trappers, from the Dura Europos find. The foreground piece is the iron trapper; the laid-out piece is the bronze example, of deeper extent and without the extended flaps to meet in front of the chest. The wiring system is shown in the top detail: convex plates are punched with four holes at the top, arranged in a square, for securing to the fabric backing; two holes at each side enable the plates to be attached to one another with wire loops.

Heavy Cavalry Armour

The Massagetae were an Iranian people with territory to the north of the Oxus and east of the Royal Scythians. During the 8th century BC one of the periodic domino movements had set the steppe nomads in motion from the hinterlands of China towards the west. The Massagetae cannoned into the Royal Scythians, driving them into the Cimmerians, who were hunted to the Greek coastal cities in Lydia, destroying Phrygia on the way. Soon after these events the Massagetae developed armour for the mounts of part of their cavalry formations. The animals' heads were protected by a chamfron, their chests by a peytral, both of thick felt embroidered for reinforcement. A few pieces were of bronze scale armour.

Body armour is often found in Scythian graves, made up of various shaped plates cut from sheet metal and mounted on a fabric backing; some, particularly later graves contain complete suits of this armour. This increasing use of armour by cavalrymen was brought about by a number of factors, the most important of which was the breeding of a weight-carrying horse using the Nisaean breed of Persia. The eastern neighbours of the Bactrians, the settled Turanians, kept these horses carefully behind the walls of Er-shih. The breed was destined to carry super-heavy cavalrymen throughout Asia in the centuries to come. The nearest living example is said to be the Akal-Teke, a sub-breed of the Turkoman standing between 15 and 16 hands. This horse, although tall, does not compare well with those depicted on Persian reliefs, which appear much bulkier. (Opinions still differ regarding the type of horse used by heavy Iranian cavalry. The examples shown throughout Iranian art associated with noble warriors are thickset, but reduced in scale. Iranian artists were quite capable of depicting a lighter horse, and convention may have dictated the thick-bodied look; but it is possible that the powerful chargers depicted were indeed being used by our subjects. The horses strongly resemble some modern medium-heavy breeds, especially the Irish cob, standing about 15–16hh, with a convex face, strong arched neck, powerful shoulders and hindquarters, short, thick boned legs and neat, strong feet.)

Soon, armour for the new type of heavy cavalry was being constructed from rawhide, horn, iron and bronze cut into scales. Some horse-trappers were of thick felt, which was possibly dyed in colours somewhat similar to those shown in medieval Persian graphic art.

In his *Anabasis*, Xenophon describes Persian cavalry armour of the 4th century BC: he says that the troopers had a helmet, cuirasse and thigh armour, and that the horses had frontlets for the head (chamfrons) and chest defences (peytrals). Greek cavalry armour included many pieces known to the later Parthians and Sassanids. The Attalid bas-reliefs on the temple of Athena Polias Nikophoros, commemorating the victories over the Gauls and built in the 2nd century BC, include a masked helmet and laminated vambraces.

The panoply of this super-heavy cavalry was extremely expensive, and varied between individuals. Any degree of standardisation may only have been present among the royal guard and retainers of some of the greater nobles. Broadly speaking, more easily obtainable materials were used for armour by early Parthian and Sassanian knights, as well as by those throughout the period who could not afford the more expensive metal armours.

The standard turn-out would have included helmets of bronze or iron, sometimes with a neck guard and/or an aventail of lamellar, scale or mail, sometimes sporting a small plume of horsehair, either dyed or left natural; and a corselet of lamellar, mail or scale for the torso. Arm guards, vambraces and rerebraces of laminated armour were made up of strips of varying size usually riveted to inner straps (as were Roman armours of segmented type). Complete laminated arm guards (*manica*), encasing the arms from the shoulder down to the knuckles, were also used. Gauntlets, reinforced with mail or small plates of metal, were worn with some armours. Thigh guards (cuisses) were of lamellar or laminated armour; leg defences (chausses) of laminated armour, though some full-length chausses were of mail. The feet were often protected by laminated armour over mail 'socks' (jambs). Mail was often used to bridge defences at limb joints. A small fabric tabard and/or cloak might be worn, and this was very likely to be made of a rich material such as silk brocade.

The primary weapon was the 12-foot lance known as the *kontos*. It had a large sword-like blade and a butt spike. Secondary weapons included a long sword, axe, mace and dagger. The *kontos* was used in a downward-stabbing overarm motion, or in both hands, as in bayonet fighting.

The panoply could be completed by horse-defences such as those previously-mentioned Hellenic armours shown on the Attalid bas-reliefs on the temple of Athena Polias Nikophoros. There is evidence for both the half-trapper, covering the chest and shoulder only, and the full trapper defending the animal's whole trunk. Neck and head were also armoured. It should be stressed, however, that horse armour was not always used by these heavy troopers.

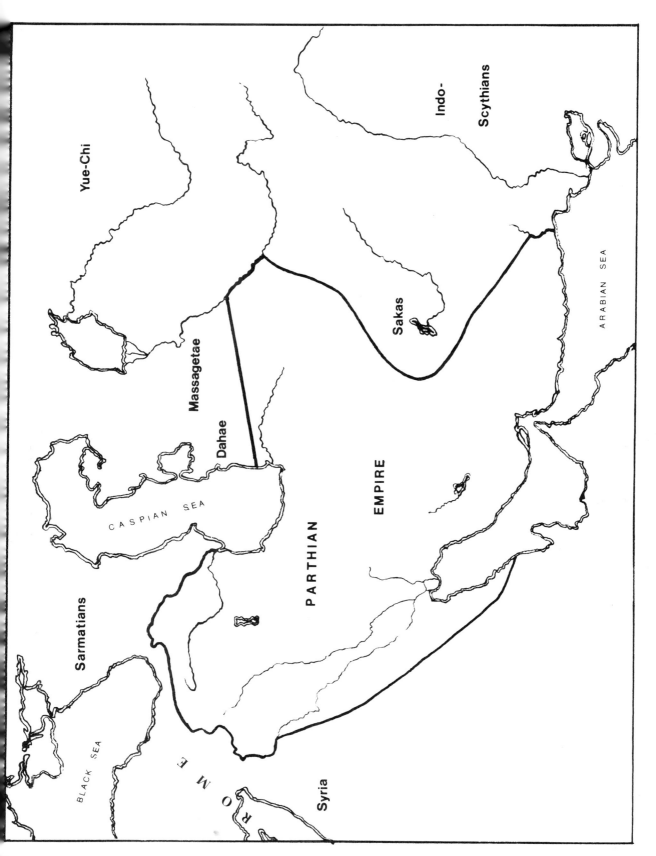

The Parthian Empire.

Yue-Chi

Indo-

Scythians

ARABIAN SEA

Massagetae

Sakas

Dahae

CASPIAN SEA

EMPIRE

PARTHIAN

Sarmatians

BLACK SEA

R
O
M
E

Syria

Horse Archers

Of the two great divisions of Parthian armies, the horse-archers were the most spectacular and traditional. These formations were manned by the less well-off petty nobility and their followers. Varying numbers of mounted bowmen from the Iranian tribes of the steppes were also used from time to time.

Parthian horse-archers were dressed in a variation of Scythian costume consisting of a leather or felt *kaftan* neatly finished off with a plain or ornate border of varying width, embroidered or in appliqué; this was of wrap-over design, held by a waist belt. Richly decorated trousers were tucked into ankle boots, which were also decorated in some cases. Wide chap-like over trousers were attached by two suspenders at the back; they were very baggy, and hung to form tightly draped folds around the legs. These may have been worn as protection for the patterned trousers. Later Parthians, from about the 1st century AD, seem to have preferred to show off their carefully tonsured hair, usually only wearing a fillet of thick ribbon; before then, the Scythian cap or *bashlyk* was worn

Major areas and cities in ancient Iran.

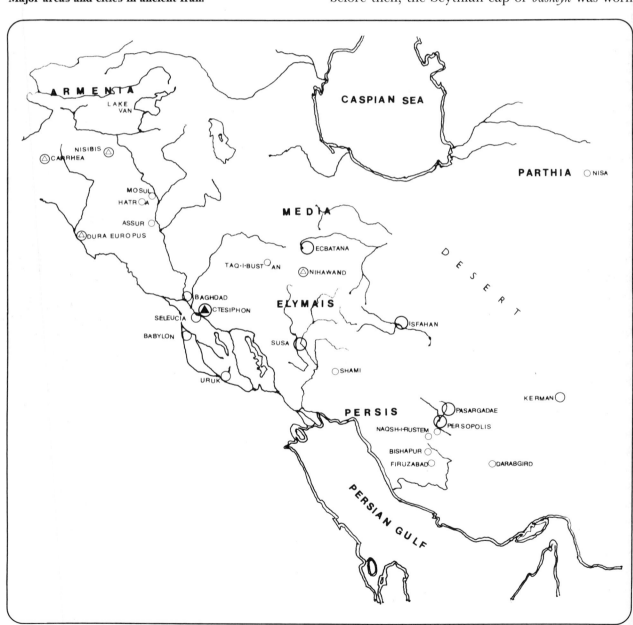

more frequently. The bow was slung from the waist belt on the left side in a case, together with a supply of arrows.

Light horse-archers could attack in various ways: arrows were carried in the left or bow hand, and one was knocked ready for release. At a signal, the assault would begin at a walk, later breaking into a canter and gallop. The arrows were released at the gallop when within range. At about 45m from the enemy front the archers swerved to the right and galloped out to the flank, shooting into the enemy lines. A more spectacular tactic was performed by bringing the mount to a skidding half-turn: as the bowmen galloped away arrows were shot over the horse's rump. Firing from this position became known as a 'Parthian' shot. If circumstances were such that the enemy could be surrounded, as at Carrhae, horse-archers were able to kill at leisure, if well led. Islamic archery manuals give quite a number of firing directions and positions possible for mounted bowmen, and it is reasonable to suppose that earlier bowmen used the same methods prior to the Arab conquests.

The primary weapon of these light cavalrymen was the powerful, recurved, composite bow constructed of layers of horn, wood and sinew. The wooden core formed the frame and was relatively 'neutral'. The strips of buffalo horn were laid on the inside to resist compression. The sinew—dried, broken into fibres, saturated in glue and layered on the outside—resisted tension. In this way tremendous energy was stored during the draw and unleashed at the release. The ears of Parthian and Sassanian bows were extended and stiffened with horn, which increased tension and controlled the release.

Arrows were about 30 ins long and were stowed in a combined quiver and bowcase of careful design, known to the Greeks as a *gorytos*; it was common to all Scythian bowmen, and was of varied construction. Some Scythian examples are faced with ornate gold or gilded silver plates of Greek workmanship. Separate bowcases and quivers of cylindrical shape were used by later Parthians and Sassanids.

To facilitate the smooth loosing of the arrow a horned thumb ring was used from about 200 BC; this allowed the string to ride smoothly over the polished surface during the release without chafing the skin. These rings were made of various hard materials, and many later examples are minor works of art in their own right. Axes, short swords, daggers and sometimes long swords were secondary weapons worn at the belt.

Islamic art of a later period shows drums carried by asses and camels, which may have followed Parthian and Sassanian tradition. Although elephants seem to play no part in the Parthian army, they were often used by the Sassanids. Standards were of a wide variety of shapes and sizes. Parthian examples would most probably include the dragon standard, designed like a wind sock; others, reproduced for Persia's 2,500 anniversary celebrations during the reign of the late Shah, included horses, moon and star, a large ear of corn, a Mithras and a sun standard.

Iranian costume: these sketches are taken from small bone plaques carved in low relief, 2nd century AD. They serve to show the basic dress of Iranian nomads on the central Asian steppes north-east of the Black Sea.

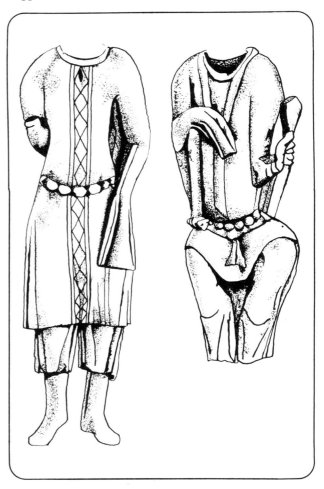

Parthian Campaigns

The weakness of the Seleucids left them powerless to deal with the growing strength and constant encroachment of the Iranians in the east, or with the Roman presence in western Asia. During the reign of Antiochus II (261–246 BC) Bactria began to show signs of breaking away from the Seleucids. Between 249 and 248 BC Parthia and Hyrcania seceded from the empire. Involved in the west, the king was unable to enforce his authority. The satrapy of Bactria was a huge frontier 'march' with a border extending north of the Oxus (Amu Daria) River. It

Two pairs of segmented arm defences carved on the ballustrade of the Temple of Athena commemorating the victories of Attalos I over his Greek and Gaulish enemies; and inner and outer views of a bronze thigh defence reconstructed from the shattered plates found at the Roman fort of Newstead in Scotland, by Russell Robinson. The former are part of a display of Greek cavalry armour; the latter would have been articulated on goatskin leather straps and would originally have had waist and thigh straps and a lining. These carefully reconstructed defences are reasonably adequate examples of the type of segmented armour also shown in much early Iranian art.

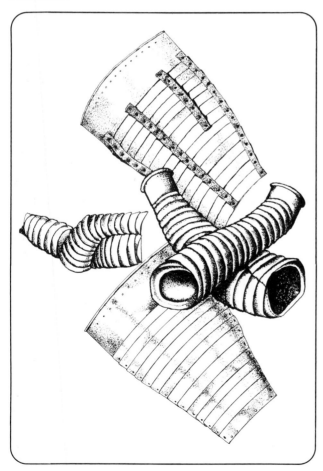

had been established to guard against the constant threat of the Iranian nomads: Alexander had settled 20,000 sick and wounded soldiers in new towns in the province during the 4th century BC. When Parthia seceded from the empire the Bactrians, now cut off from central authority, also seceded (248 BC).

When Seleucus II (246–226 BC) marched east to restore the situation the Parthians, a fluid and flexible people, retreated in good order at his approach; a serious uprising in Syria forced the king to abandon his campaign and return west, and the Parthians returned, the 'victors'. After the death of Seleucus II in 226 BC the shrinking Seleucid Empire also lost territories in Asia Minor.

Antiochus III (223–187 BC) was an energetic and sophisticated ruler. On his accession to the Seleucid throne he was faced with a revolt by the satraps of Media and Persis, and by the threat of the Parthians, now allied to the Bactrians, hanging over Media. Antiochus set out from Antioch, crushed the satraps, and marched east on an armed progress that lasted eight years. After crossing the whole of Iran from north to south he returned to Ecbatana to harry the Parthians (209 BC); the Parthian king Ardavan Artabanus I (214–196) led his people in the time-honoured orderly Parthian retreat, but finally submitted and brought tribute. Bactria was attacked, but put up a stiff defence at the border, leading to a treaty of friendship.

Encouraged by his success Antiochus marched west and crossed the straits to Greece; but Roman forces drove him back to Lydia—where they destroyed his army in the crushing defeat at Magnesia in 190 BC. The subsequent treaty, agreed in 188 BC, deprived Antiochus of Seleucid possessions in Asia Minor and imposed a massive tribute. Antiochus III died the following year.

The last Seleucid king of any note was Antiochus IV (175–164 BC); shortly after his death the oriental territories of the Seleucid Empire began to fragment into petty states, lacking cohesion and open to Parthian conquest. Roman policy had destroyed Seleucid power but had indirectly prepared the way for the rapid growth of the Iranian threat.

Between 160 and 140 BC the Parthian king, Mithridates I, the founder of the Parthian Empire, annexed Media, Elymais, Persis, Characene, Babylonia, Assyria, Gedrosia, and probably Herat and Seistan in the east. The great commercial centre of Seleucia city on the Tigris controlled much of the Iranians' international trade, and during the Parthian takeover the Greco-Semitic oligarchy seem to have reached a mutually satisfactory agreement with their new masters, persuading the Parthians to avoid settling the city. Instead, a huge nomad-type camp was erected on the opposite bank of the Tigris; in due time this became Ctesiphon, capital of Parthia.

The old Iranian territories offered stiff resistance, and never fully accepted Parthian supremacy despite the adoption by Mithridates of the ancient title of King of Kings. Greek misgivings were soothed by the inclusion of the word 'Philhellene' on Parthian coinage; but the Parthians had no friends in Persia. When Demetrius II took a resurrected Seleucid army of sorts into the new Parthian territories in 138 BC he was offered help by Seleucia city, Elymais, Persis and Greco-Bactria. Demetrius was defeated in the war which followed, but when captured he was treated with respect, and sent to Hyrcania with the Parthian king's daughter as his wife. Elymais was made the scapegoat for this episode, and in revenge its richer temples were put to sack by the Parthians.

Mithridates I died in 137 BC. In 129 BC a last attempt to regain the lost provinces and free Demetrius was made when his brother Antiochus VII Sidates took a strong, well-trained Seleucid army into Mesopotamia. Here he was successful in a series of three pitched battles against the new Parthian king Phraates II, whose semi-professional feudal army proved no match for the trained Seleucid troops. However, the predatory behaviour of Antiochus' troops antagonised the local population of the city and surroundings of Ecbatana where they were quartered. Encouraged by Parthian agents, the people rose in revolt: a simultaneous Parthian attack routed the Seleucids, and Antiochus was killed. Eventually, elements of his army were inducted into that of the Parthians.

Seleucid influence in Iran was immediately forfeit, and Parthia stood fully armed at the Euphrates. At this point Parthian attention had to be switched to the eastern flank, where Scythian nomads—final victims of a vast movement on the steppes, which had forced Iranians to move from territories in Chinese Turkestan—began to pour

Parthian iron helmet of the 3rd century AD, of 'spangenhelm' construction: it is made up of four iron plates secured to four inverted 'T'-shaped pieces with domed rivets; a small oblong plate at the apex holds a small round finial. The headband is wrapped around the lower section and fixed in place with a row of ball rivets. (Trustees of the British Museum)

into Parthian territory in about 140 BC. One group headed towards Merv, Hecatompolis, and Ecbatana. Their first attack caused the newly-incorporated Greek troops to desert, bringing about the defeat and death of Phraates (138–124 BC). Artabanus II, his uncle, succeeded him, but was also killed by the Scythians in 123 BC.

The governor of Babylonia, declaring himself king of Characene, broke away from Parthia. In 123 BC Mithridates II became king of Parthia, and quickly brought the governor of Babylonia to heel. In the east he rolled the Scythians back to the Oxus, beyond which the nomads settled to become marcher tribes of the Parthian Empire, where they functioned as buffers against their nomadic brothers, the Sakae tribesmen.

Greco-Bactria was obliterated. The middle Oxus was now occupied by two great Iranian 'super-tribes', the Sacaraucae and the Yueh-Chi (Kushans) who had been driven from the Chinese frontier. By the 1st century BC both groups were established in Bactria, where they became closely linked with Parthian culture and politics.

In the late 2nd century BC Mithridates II received an important embassy from the Emperor of China. During negotiations a treaty was concluded for the free movement of merchandise throughout Greater Parthia as a transit state for international trade.

The consolidation and organisation of Parthian Iran during the reign of Mithridates II was followed after his death in 87 BC by internal strife. Tigranes, the puppet king of Armenia, seized the occasion to declare himself King of Kings, and annexed other provinces to the south, including Ecbatana. The Syrians, bored with Seleucid squabbling, offered the Seleucid crown to Tigranes, who accepted, and prepared for his next political move.

Rome, still anxious to keep the Parthians out of western Asian politics, looked for neutrality treaties. These were given by Phraates III, and were

Detail figure of a barbarian returning an *aquilla* standard to a Roman officer, from the muscle cuirass on the Prima Porta statue of Augustus. The scene is believed to show Tiberius accepting one of the standards captured at Carrhae from a Parthian in c. 20 BC. (Vatican Museum)

scrupulously honoured. Within a few years Pompey had violated the treaties, seizing the western provinces of Parthia and plotting with the princes of vassal states. When Phraates objected he was insulted by Pompey. Following the assassination of Phraates III in 57 BC, the Romans intrigued to assist Mithridates III (58–55 BC) to keep the throne from Orodes I (56–37 BC) but eventually they failed.

The rapacity of Rome was well demonstrated when, in 53 BC, at the age of 60, Marcus Licinius Crassus took up his proconsular duties in Syria. Excited by his new acquisition and hot from the power politics of Rome, this ambitious aristocrat accepted the command of the army of the east, and prepared for a series of conquests which would equal those of Alexander the Great. He was indeed to achieve a secure place in the history books: but for rather different reasons.

Carrhae, 53 BC

No war with Parthia was contemplated by the tamed Senate, but objections they raised against Crassus' plans were brushed aside. Julius Caesar was full of encouragement; but Crassus had left Rome with religious curses from Aetius, a tribune, ringing in his ears. It was argued that the Parthians were protected by a valid neutrality treaty with Rome, and could therefore expect to be safe from Roman attack.

The first offensive act by Crassus was to cross the Euphrates and leave Roman garrisons in several Mesopotamian cities, which gave him willing allegiance. The city of Zenodotia resisted, but its defences were destroyed, the citizens plundered and enslaved. Crassus withdrew to winter in Syria and to await his son, Publius, who was on his way with 1,000 crack Gaulish cavalrymen.

In the spring Crassus massed seven legions, 4,000 auxiliary infantrymen and 3,000 western Asian auxiliary cavalrymen, who were joined by the 1,000 Gallic troopers. Disturbing reports of Parthian military efficiency began arriving at the Roman martialling area from the garrisons left in the Mesopotamian cities. They were mostly exaggerated but, in essence, were to prove prophetic.

King Artavasdes of Armenia arrived at the Roman camp with 6,000 troopers and a promise of 10,000 cavalrymen and 30,000 infantry. The king advised Crassus to march into Parthia by way of the foothills of southern Armenia where enemy cavalrymen, particularly of the cataphract type, could operate only with great difficulty; the region was well watered, and supplies would be guaranteed. Crassus, however, decided to take the more direct desert route into Parthia, with Seleucia city and Ctesiphon as his objectives. Eventually, in the spring of 53 BC, the Roman army of the east crossed the River Euphrates near the town of Zeugma during a heavy storm.

After a difficult crossing, and dogged by bad omens (the Romans were extremely superstitious), they marched south close to the river while the area to the east was reconnoitred. The scouts reported no troops in the immediate vicinity, but found tracks of many horsemen.

While Crassus considered alternative routes, Ariamnes, a treacherous Nabataen Arab chieftain from Edessa, set about his secret task of getting Crassus to take the desert, rather than the securer river route to Seleucia. He argued that no Parthian force of any strength was nearby, and that forced desert marches would enable the Romans to catch up with the fleeing enemy who had left the tracks found by Roman scouts, and who would be burdened with slaves and impedimenta. The Romans were told that the only troops who might attempt to bar their way were an advance guard under Surena. Crassus decided to allow the Arabs to lead his army into the desert (Ariamnes and Alchaudonius, another chieftain from Edessa, had a following of 6,000 Arab light troopers).

The Parthian king, Orodes II, had decided to split his army in two. The king led one contingent into Armenia, where he burned villages and harried

A terracotta plaque showing a Parthian cataphract hunting lion, holding his lance in both hands. (Trustees of the British Museum)

Parthian horse-archer on a terracotta plaque. He is shown at half-draw, his legs clenched tightly to his pony's belly, with an interesting bowcase slung from his belt: it holds a spare unstrung bow, arrows, and a short sword in a scabbard at the front of the case. See Plate B3. (Trustees of the British Museum)

the countryside to punish King Artavasdes for involving Armenia in military preparations directed against Parthia in alliance with Rome. The second contingent was commanded by Surena, the senior male member of the most powerful of the seven great clans of Parthia. Known as The Surena, he led a force composed almost completely of his own troops. Most of his horse-archers were from the Saka and the Yue-Chi people. Surena had a reputation for intelligent leadership. He was tall, handsome, and—according to Plutarch—wore make-up on the battlefield: this may have been *kohl*, applied to the cheeks to cut down glare into the eyes, as used by modern Bedouin. His force was most probably sent to the Euphrates, as nothing more than a powerful probe to delay the Romans until Orodes had finished his Armenian raid, and was able to attempt the destruction of the Roman force with a bigger proportion of the Parthian army.

The Romans were led away from the Euphrates towards open, featureless desert. At first they passed through pleasant riverine semi-cultivated country,

but this vegetation gradually dwindled into desert, and marching for the infantry became increasingly difficult. At this time of low morale messengers from King Artavasdes brought the news that the Armenian troops promised to Crassus could not be sent due to the pressure of Orodes' attack on Armenia. Crassus was strongly advised to join forces with Artavasdes in Armenia or, failing that, to take the foothill route. This second warning to keep away from the open country which favoured Parthian cavalry was brushed aside by Crassus, who told the messengers that when he had more time he would make their king pay for his treachery.

As the punishing march was resumed the Arab chieftain, Ariamnes, put the finishing touches to his duplicity by chivvying the Roman troops over the cautious pace of their advance; then, convincing the Roman officers that they wished to disrupt and confuse the Parthian army, the Arab leaders rode away with their 6,000 followers. Plutarch says that at this point Crassus made his infantry march at cavalry pace.

As they neared the ancient town of Carrhae (now known as Haran) Roman vedettes began to return from their posts in advance of the column, reporting that some of the Roman cavalry screen had been killed by Parthians, whose main force was now deploying ahead for an immediate engagement. According to Plutarch, Crassus seems to have been caught completely unawares and began to show signs of panic, giving hasty and unconsidered orders. Cassius, a staff officer, stepped in to advise him to extend the infantry in its line of battle across the plain, dividing the cavalry between the wings. These manoeuvres were underway when Crassus changed his mind and gave orders for the legions to go into hollow square with 12 cohorts on each side, each with cavalry and light infantry support. Crassus took position inside the huge square together with his guard and the Gallic cavalry commanded by his son Publius, and the baggage train.

·In this formation Crassus gave the order to advance. After some time the little Ballisur stream was reached. Crassus was advised to stop here for the night, engaging the enemy the next day after assessing their strength; but Publius and his Gauls were impatient for action, and Crassus was persuaded to press on. He gave orders for the men to be fed and watered as they stood in the gigantic square, but most had not finished their meal when Crassus gave the order to advance without rest until the enemy were sighted.

When the Parthian army came into full view they seemed to the Romans neither impressive nor numerous. Plutarch says that Surena had hidden his main force behind the front ranks. It seems that the Roman troops had expected to see Parthian cataphracts in complete armour, and were pleasantly surprised when none seemed to be present. Surena had evidently told his cataphracts to cover themselves with coats and hides so as to hide their glittering armour. As the Roman troops reached the battleground and stood ready for action Surena gave a signal, and the air was filled with the loud throbbing of large drums, with attached bronze bells, from positions all over the battlefield. At this moment the cataphracts dropped the covers from their armour. Plutarch says: 'Now they could be seen clearly, their helmets and breastplates blazing like fire, their Margianian steel glittering keen and bright, their horses armoured with plates of bronze and steel.' (Margiania was an old satrapy of the earlier Achaemenid Empire, straddling the trade route between Merv and Seleucia city on the Tigris. Plutarch also calls Parthian armour the 'arms of Merv': it is almost certain that Merv was importing the high-quality steel of Pliny's famed Seres, the tall, flaxen-haired, blue-eyed nomads 'who speak in harsh tones and use no language', and that

The Eastern Roman Empire, 4th century AD, showing the prefectures of Illyria and the East. Black squares show legionary garrisons; larger squares, mobile field armies.

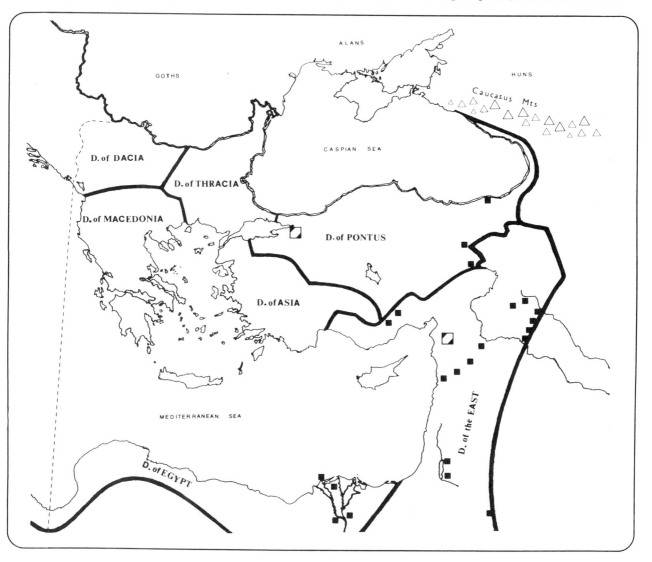

Margiania gave the steel a geographical name.)

Surena seems to have planned to break the Roman square with a charge by his 1,000 cataphracts, so that the horse-archers could attack a disordered enemy. This plan was quickly changed when he discovered the depth of the Roman lines: the cataphracts withdrew, and the horse-archers began to envelop the square.

A charge by some Roman light infantry achieved nothing; the horse-archers merely withdrew, peppering the auxiliary infantry with arrows and driving them back into the square. The Romans became aware that Parthian arrows could punch through their armour and shields as the arrow-storm began to fall among the packed ranks of the square. The Romans clung to the hope that this phase of the battle would peter out as Parthian quivers emptied. Hope was shattered when it was seen that some horse-archers were returning from an ammunition train of camels with replenished quivers.

Seeing his rear about to be attacked, Crassus put together an assault force of the Gallic cavalry, 300 light troopers, 500 foot archers and eight cohorts of the legions under the command of his son Publius, with orders to attack the gathering Parthian bowmen. As the Roman force advanced the horse-archers turned and galloped away. Publius was taken in, and followed in pursuit, losing sight of the Roman main body. After some time the Parthians wheeled about, now joined by a larger Parthian force including cataphracts. The Romans halted,

and were promptly attacked by horse-archers darting in and out. Publius led the Gauls in an attack on the cataphracts. Although the Gallic spears failed to penetrate Parthian armour, the Gauls bravely pressed home their attack, grabbing the enemy's long lances, pulling the riders to the ground, and scrambling under the horses' bellies to stab them. They even drove their own mounts on to the long Parthian lances. The Gauls were eventually forced to retire with the wounded Publius to a small hillock, where they were surrounded and attacked. About 500 of them were taken prisoner; Publius was killed, and his head was cut off. The Parthian troops rode back to Surena's main force.

Crassus, noticing that pressure on his square had slackened, and unaware of the disaster overtaking Publius and his force, relocated his army on sloping ground in conventional battle order. After several of Publius' messengers had been killed, others got through to tell Crassus of his son's predicament. Crassus sent no support, but began an advance. Again Parthian drums began to throb, and Surena had Publius' head paraded in front of Roman lines on a spear. The advance was stopped by the bowmen and cataphracts. When night fell the Parthians offered Crassus his life if he would surrender, giving him the night to mourn the death of his son.

During the night Crassus lost self control, and it fell to his two subordinates to call a staff meeting. The agreed action was to leave the wounded and retreat under cover of night. The cavalry, on hearing the decision, decided to leave forthwith to avoid the chaos of a night retreat. As they passed the town of Carrhae they told the sentries on the wall of the disaster, and rode on to Zeugma.

The Parthians quietly watched the Roman retreat without interfering. They slaughtered the wounded left in the Roman camp. Crassus and the remains of the Roman army reached Carrhae, and were taken into safety. Some time later four legionary cohorts commanded by Vargontuis, who had strayed from the main Roman column during the retreat, were surrounded and destroyed; 20 survivors were allowed to march to Carrhae, in compliment to the boldness they had shown in attempting to hack their way to freedom through the Parthian ranks.

A Parthian cataphract resting; this rather ambiguous little terracotta figure shows the soldier in full armour but bare-headed. (Trustees of the British Museum)

Surena soon discovered that Crassus was in Carrhae with the survivors of his army. The Romans chose to escape from the city, again by night. Their guide, who was in Parthian pay, eventually led the Roman column into marshy ground. The bewildered Romans were offered the chance of truce and friendship on behalf of the king by Surena. The Roman troops forced Crassus to accept by threatening his life. During a struggle which took place at the subsequent meeting with Parthian leaders, Crassus was killed. His head and right hand were cut off. Some of the troops

Reflexed composite bow, showing main components. The sinew fibres were soaked in glue and built on to the back of the wooden core; the horn strip was glued to the belly. In the diagram of the draw (a) is unstrung shape, (b) is strung, (c) is the draw.

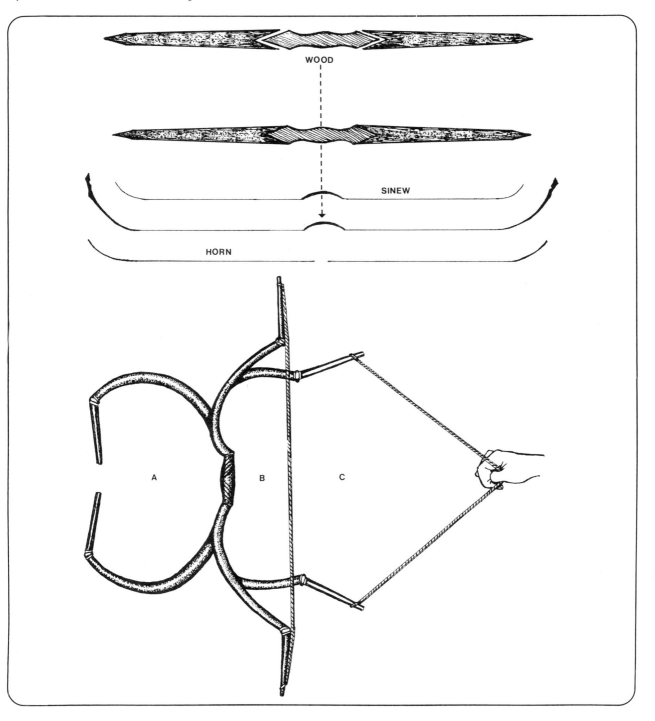

WOOD

SINEW

HORN

A   B   C

surrendered; some escaped; most were hunted and killed by scavenging Arabs. Surena's force of 1,000 cataphracts and 10,000 horse-archers had destroyed a Roman army of 28,000 legionaries, 3,000 Asian cavalry and 1,000 Gaulish cavalry. In all some 20,000 Romans lost their lives, and 10,000 were captured.

Messengers delivered the head and hand of Crassus to the palace of the king of Armenia where the Parthian king was a guest. Both kings were watching a performance of the *Bacchantes* by Euripides, an allegorical study contrasting the barbaric military practices of Asia with Hellenic culture. During the announcement of the victory the head of Crassus was tossed onto the stage: a *coup de théâtre* which the actors must have found hard to follow . . .

The captured Roman standards were laid up in Parthian temples and the prisoners, many of them skilled craftsmen, were settled in the vicinity of Merv. Very soon after his great victory, Surena was executed by order of the king who, says Plutarch, was jealous of the great general.

*　　*　　*

Carrhae was a traumatic shock for Rome and her army. Sixteen years earlier, at Tigranocerta about

80 miles north-east of Carrhae, Roman troops had met cataphracts of the Armenian army and defeated them: Lucullus' legions had taken the heavy troopers in flank, obeying orders to cut at the exposed thighs of the horses. The Armenians had hurriedly retired, taking the rest of the army with them. Now, at Carrhae, a Roman army had been methodically destroyed by horse-archers supported by a relatively small force of heavy cavalry. The Semitic merchants of the Levant began to see in the horsemen of Parthia saviours from the oppressive demands of the Roman tax collector, and gradually took on a pro-Parthian stance.

In 51 BC a Parthian army commanded by Pacorus, a prince of the royal house, made a short and disastrous raid into Syria. When a second raid, lasting several months, was attempted later that year, economic chaos resulted throughout western Asia. Pacorus was recalled to prevent further counter-productive damage; falsely accused of plotting against his father, he narrowly escaped with his life. A period of quiet on the Euphrates frontier lasted for about ten years.

In 40 BC the Parthian army was again split. Part was commanded by Labienus, a former Roman ambassador from Brutus who had wisely chosen to stay in Parthia. The other division of the army was led by the king's son Pacorus. The force led by Labienus moved to control most of Asia Minor; Pacorus pushed south into a large area of Roman

The defeat of the Parthians, 3rd century AD: these rock carvings from Firusabad, Iran, show the Persian monarch Ardashir I (AD 224–241) and his son in combat with the Parthian king Artabanus V. Here Prince Shapur is shown unhorsing the Grand Vizier of Parthia.

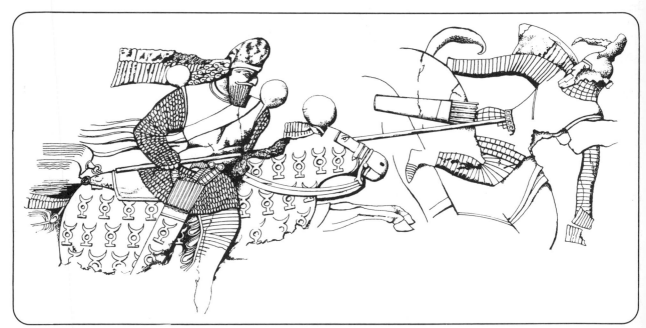

Asia. Subsequently the Parthians found it an impossible task to defend the conquered territories in the face of large numbers of Roman reinforcements. At Taurus the following year, 39 BC, the Parthian horse-archers were held at bay by massed slingers. The cataphracts were unable to break the 11 legions drawn up on rising ground. The next year, 38 BC, Pacorus suffered an absolute disaster, losing his life when he attacked what he thought to be an undefended Roman camp at Gindarus. His cataphracts, who were without horse-archers, were again fought to a standstill, and retired in some haste.

The ageing Orodes II was eventually killed by his remaining sons in 37 BC. The accession of Phraates IV was followed by dangerous in-fighting between the two great divisions of the Parthian army—the heavy formations, manned by the great landed clans, and the horse-archers, originally manned by yeomen Parthians of modest means but now diluted by landless non-Parthian Iranian nomads, which element was probably responsible for the unrest.

In 36 BC a Roman expedition led by Mark Antony followed the plan laid down by Julius Caesar 12 years earlier for the conquest of the east. It began with an invasion of Transcaucasia. Armenia became a vassal state, and the Roman force marched into Media Atropatene to lay siege to the capital, Phraaspa. A powerful siege train, trundling along at a more measured pace, was burnt and the baggage plundered when the column was attacked by the Parthians, led by Phraates IV. The siege of Phraaspa failed; during the Roman withdrawal they were constantly harassed by Parthian bowmen. Mark Antony made another attempt the following year with Armenian help; but the Parthians were again able to defeat his forces.

In 27 BC Octavius Caesar, the emperor of the west, became at the age of 36 total hegamon of the Roman world and changed his name to Augustus. His summary of Parthian military capabilities was that they were capable of no sustained offensive warfare, and he resolved to compromise and reach some kind of *modus vivendi* with the great Asian nation. Strategic perimeters were regularised by re-asserting suzerainty over Transcaucasia and Armenia, and a Romanisation programme was set in motion. Negotiations with Phraates IV for the return of the standards captured at Carrhae bore

Persian knight wrestling a Parthian noble out of the saddle; carving from Firusabad, Iran. Cf. Plates D1, D2.

fruit in AD 20.

During the 1st century AD Parthia experienced a gradual Persian cultural resurgence. At the end of the century the brother of the Parthian king Vologases I was made king of Armenia, receiving his crown from Nero. With Tiridates on the Armenian throne, the Arsacid dynasty controlled both strong Asian nations.

Trajan's conquest of Armenia and Transcaucasia in AD 114 brought him to the Euphrates, which he crossed the next year. Adiabene and Mesopotamia were conquered, and Ctesiphon was taken; The Parthian king and his daughter were captured. Trajan decided to end his conquests on reaching Charax, and in AD 117 he died. The Emperor Hadrian pulled the Roman troops back to the line of the Euphrates. Ctesiphon, the Parthian capital, was subsequently captured on two other occasions. In AD 165 the palace was burnt down, but Roman troops retired when an outbreak of plague began to rage throughout Iran. In AD 197 the royal residence was again burnt down. After a series of victories over Roman forces in Parthia Artabanus V drove them back to the Euphrates, where he was able to impose a heavy tribute on the Emperor Macrinus. The attempts to bring Parthia under Roman control had failed, and a Parthian invasion of Asia Minor was imminent; but in AD 224, at Susiana, Artabanus was killed in battle against the army of the Sassanid Persians. Within two years the Sassanians had completely overthrown the Parthians.

The Parthians had ruled Persia for nearly 400 years. During their paramountcy Rome—apart from a few fleeting successes—had been held at bay for three centuries. The Parthians had also revived Iranian martial ardour, lost under the Seleucids; and acted as the vital Iranian link between the Medo-Persians of old and the Persian Sassanids.

Sassanid Persia

At the head of Sassanid society was the King of Kings. Below him were grouped the vassal princes who, after recognising the authority of the great throne, were allowed to keep their respective thrones. This stratum was duplicated by Parthian princes of the blood who governed satrapies (provinces) of great importance, such as Kerman and Seistan. These vassal princes were required to supply troops to protect the territory. They were of particular importance on the periphery of the empire, where they performed the same buffer function as the settled Germans (*feoderates*) on the northern frontier of the Roman Empire.

Next in status came the heads of the seven great clans, who followed the feudal system of their Parthian predecessors. The Sassanid kings were conscious of the part played by the Parthian aristocracy in the downfall of the Parthian Empire, and tried to curb the power of their own Sassanid clans (who would, nevertheless, eventually play an almost identical rôle in the destruction of Sassanid Persia). Some way below the noble clans, the yeoman nobles and village headmen were responsible for the supply of peasant soldiers in time of war, and for the collection of taxes. The peasants had been reduced to serfdom and were sold as part of the livestock of land and village. Ordeal and torture were tools of the state, and were of great refinement and cruelty.

Sassanid administration was headed by the Grand Vizier, who was in charge of political and diplomatic affairs. On occasion he commanded the army in the field. He also headed the *divans* (ministries), which were directed by secretaries expert in their various fields. As with the Parthians, the economy was based on agriculture. Revenue increase during the Sassanid period led gradually to a fairer redistribution of goods. Banking was well advanced. Trade was vigorous and well monitored. State monopolies rivalled private concerns; in particular, raw silk from China was woven at workshops in Susa, Gundeshapur and Shushtar. China and glass, textiles, garments, amber, papyrus and spices were imported; pepper and nard from Media, corn, cattle and manufactured goods were exported. Controls were extremely stringent where industry dealt with state organisations such as the army, court and administration.

The power of the nobles during the Sassanian period grew at an alarming rate. Towards the end of the period their position was so strong that the king was totally dependent on them, financially and militarily. As in the Roman Empire, the great estates became enclosed enclaves guarded by private garrisons against the possibility of an uprising of the peasantry. Life was good to the cultured, land-owning nobility. They elected the king, and enjoyed certain hereditary privileges. Their lives were filled with martial training, hunting, feasting, the enjoyment of women, literature, chess, tennis, polo, music, singing and graphic art. The descriptions of early travellers and historians, and the evidence of archaeology, agree in ascribing to the Sassanid monarchy and nobility a dazzling richness of architectural decoration, costume, and jewellery.

The Sassanian Army

During the first three centuries of Sassanid rule the Persian army was headed by one commander-in-chief, a hereditary office held by a member of the royal family. The great clans filled the posts of adjutant-general and commander of cavalry. Chosroes I (AD 531–79) eventually undermined the power of the army commander by placing the four

1, 2: Parthian cataphracts, 1st century BC

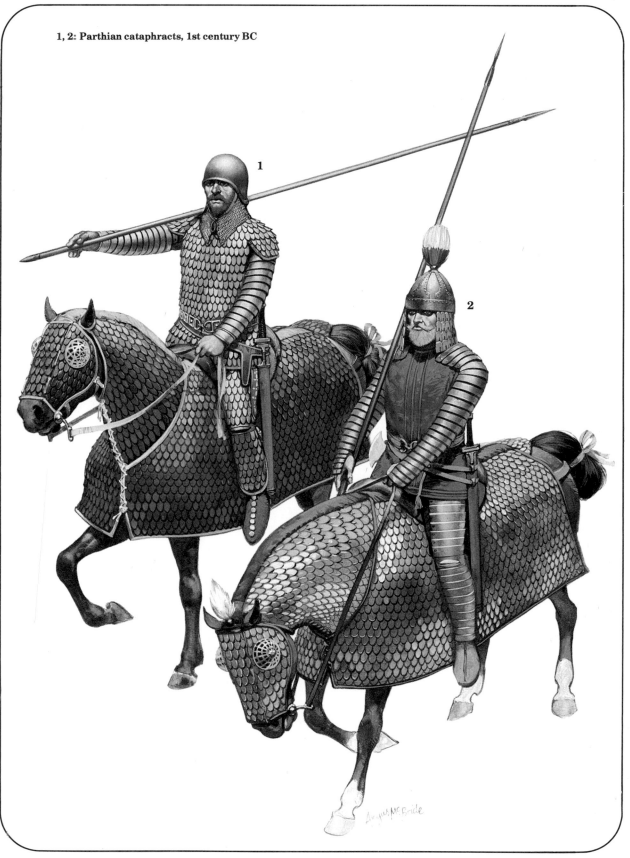

A

1: Early Parthian horse-archer, 4th C. BC
2: Parthian horse-archer, 2nd century BC
3: Parthian horse-archer, 3rd century AD

1: Parthian cataphract, 2nd century AD
2: Armenian cataphract, 3rd century AD

C

1: Early Sassanian cataphract, 3rd C. AD
2: Parthian cataphract, 3rd C. AD
3: Sassanian standard-bearer

3

1

2

1: Sassanian clibanarius, 6th C. AD
2: Sassanian war elephant

E

1: Nomadic Iranian horse-archer
2: Chionite-Ephthalite horse-archer
3: Nomadic standard-bearer

F

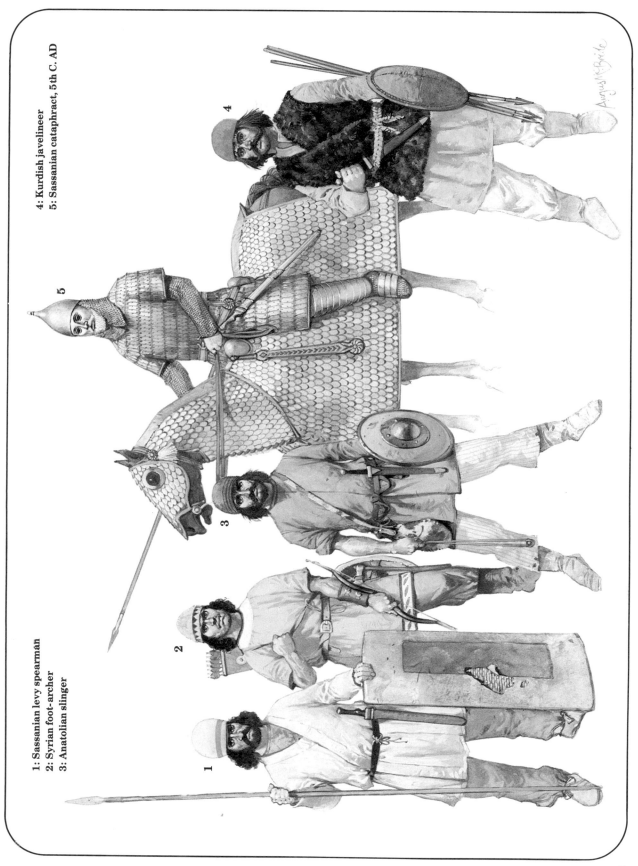

1: Sassanian levy spearman
2: Syrian foot-archer
3: Anatolian slinger

4: Kurdish javelineer
5: Sassanian cataphract, 5th C. AD

G

1: Sassanian clibanarius, 7th C. AD
2: Sassanian standard-bearer

AngusMcBride

H

cardinal divisions of the empire under the protection of four local commanders, each with a deputy.

The Sassanid army was divided into corps which were split into divisions and these in turn were divided into brigades. The military system inherited from the Parthians was based on the heavy, armoured cavalry provided by the aristocracy, and the light horse-archers provided by the minor nobility and nomad mercenaries. Elephants were usually placed in the rear; they would have been of Indian type, with *howdahs* carrying armed soldiers and a driver. The bulk of the peasant infantry were forced into the field, and formed the rear guard: they were next to useless as soldiers, poorly armed and of low morale. When they were not being used as spearmen they were engaged in duties around the camp. Better-quality infantry were found in the ranks of the slingers and foot-archers. The superb horsemen of the steppes swelled the ranks of horse-archers. These auxiliary formations were sent from the northern and eastern borderlands of the empire, including Iranians from Seistan and Kushan, Albans and Mongolian Chionite-Ephthalites. Armenian troops were highly regarded; their heavy and light formations occupied an honoured position in the Sassanid army.

The Sassanids were very good at sieges, a skill not possessed by the Parthians. As mentioned above, some frontiers were guarded by colonies of warlike subjects, peoples settled in a given area who would take the first shock of any invasion attempt until the regular army took the field. Military technical literature was produced, and is known indirectly from Arabic sources; treatises dealing with organisation, care of horses, riding, archery, tactics and victualling are known to have existed.

Elite units of the Sassanid army were probably armed in the full panoply of the *clibanarius* on the battlefield. The unit known as 'The Immortals' numbered about 10,000; a deliberate emulation of the unit of the same name and function in the Achaemenid Persian army, defeated by Alexander the Great, this seems to have been instituted at an early date in Sassanid history. Little is known of another unit bearing the name Gyanarspar ('Sacrificers of their lives'). The imperial bodyguard, the Pushtighban, numbered 6,000 at the beginning of the 7th century AD.

During the period from the beginning of the rise of Parthia to the Arab conquests of Sassanian Persia there seems to have been no significant change in the armament of the two classic divisions of the armies of Iran. The acceptance of Persians within the ranks of noble Parthian heavy cavalry, at least towards the latter part of the Parthian period, is evidenced by the military preparedness of the nobles of Fars who were able to challenge the Parthian army on an equal footing, fully armoured and bow-armed. To what extent individual Parthian nobles were removed from power in the new Sassanian Empire cannot be judged. Some powerful Parthian nobles willing to accept Sassanian overlordship were left in possession of their estates and were ranked with the princes of the royal blood and high Persian aristocrats. In time of war both Parthian and Persian nobles would present themselves and their vassals for service as part of the metropolitan army of Iran.

As mentioned above, the arming of Iran remained unaltered in its broad aspect for centuries. Variations, such as the absence of trappers for the mounts of Parthian or Sassanian *clibanarii*, did not always signify lack of funds, although increasing affluence would allow for a proportional increase in the quantity and quality of armour. Military fashion did vary slightly in the 4th century AD, when formations of heavier armoured troops were developed to operate with Sassanian *clibanarii*, but these do not seem to have lasted beyond the 5th century.

Armour

In his *Aethiopica*, written in the 3rd century AD, Heliodorus says that Persian heavy cavalry were encased completely in bronze or iron, with a one-piece masked helmet entirely covering the head except for the eyes. The description is repeated in the writings of Ammianus Marcellinus, who lived during the 4th century AD: '. . . Moreover all the companies were clad in iron, and all parts of their bodies were covered with thick plates, so fitted that the stiff joints conformed with those of their limbs; and the forms of human faces were so skilfully fitted to their head that, since their entire bodies were covered in metal, arrows that fell upon them could lodge only where they could see a little through tiny openings opposite the pupil of the eye, or where

Sassanian helmet of 3rd century AD; this conical iron headpiece is very similar in shape to those used by Assyrian troops. It is constructed of four triangular iron plates brought together and reinforced by four waisted, spear-shaped iron straps secured with ball rivets. The apex has not survived, but may have been a rounded point, or a hollow finial housing a plume. Rusted rings of iron mail have fused to the rim. (Trustees of the British Museum)

through the tips of their noses they were able to get a little breath'; and 'The Persians opposed to us serried bands of mail-clad horsemen in such close order that the gleam of moving bodies covered with closely fitting plates of iron dazzled the eyes of those who looked upon them, while the whole throng of horses was protected by coverings of leather'.

The Persians were excellent armourers and were recognised throughout Asia as leaders in this field for centuries. (Although it is most probable that the armours spoken of by Xenophon were very similar to the Greek examples of a slightly later date).

The terms *cataphract* and *clibanarius* are used to describe ancient super-heavy cavalrymen. The first is derived from the Greek *cataphractoi*, meaning 'covered over'. (The Latin term *cataphractus* was, however, often used for the Roman heavy cavalryman of the 2nd and 3rd centuries AD, who was armoured only with helmet and corselet.) By the 3rd century Rome had adopted the full panoply of the super-heavy trooper. The word *clibanarius* is variously said to derive from the old Persian *griv-pan*, meaning 'warrior'; from *grivpan*, the Pahlavi name for the pendant mail helmet defence; or from the Latin for a field oven, *clibanus*, in a joking

reference to these troopers sweltering in full armour in Mediterranean climates.

Most Oriental mail was made in much the same way as that of Europe: wire was drawn, wound around a rod and cut into little rings, the ends then being flattened, punched, linked to four others, and riveted. Older armours were made of alternate rows of riveted wire rings and rings punched from sheet metal. Scale armour was made up of small plates cut from sheets of bronze or iron, and sometimes spined or bossed by means of a punch to give rigidity. They were laced together through pierced holes and mounted on a tough fabric or fine leather garment. Lamellar, a near relative of scale armour, was made up of small rectangular plates cut from a number of animal or metallic substances. These were pierced, and laced together with wire rawhide thongs in rows to the length required. The rows were then laced vertically, with the plates overlapping upwards. Simplicity and speed of manufacture made this defence popular throughout Asia up to the 19th century.

During the 1930s French and American excavations at Dura Europos on the Euphrates—a fortified city occupied in turn by Greeks, Parthians, Romans and Sassanid Persians—some interesting pieces of armour were brought to light. In Tower 19, which had been mined by the Persians, the skeleton of a Persian trooper was found complete with a hip-length mail corselet with short sleeves, and a 'thimble-shaped' helmet. Nearby was a rectangular cane shield.

Remains of three horse armours were found: all are trappers or bards, two of them complete. These are made respectively of iron and bronze scales of varying size, which are looped together with pieces of wire in rows set one over the other, and sewn onto a strong, rough, linen-type fabric. They are bound at the edges with red rawhide. The trappers are open at the front and rear and have a triangular process at rear-centre, corresponding with the horse's tail base. There is a large central oval hole to allow for the saddle. Following the spinal area is a broad rawhide panel holding the two plated areas together. (The third trapper was extremely decayed and fragmentary.)

Two cuisses of rawhide lamellar were also found and, in the opinion of the late Russell Robinson, may have been part of the equipment of a Parthian auxiliary unit attached to the Roman garrison at the time of Dura's seizure by the Persians in AD 256. Both are tinted with a sanderac lacquer finish, one red, one black; both are surface-laced with red rawhide thongs.

Evidence for the construction and appearance of a metal cuisse was found at Newstead fort, a Roman stronghold on Tweedside, near Melrose in Scotland. The crystalline pieces were placed together and the cuisse was reconstructed by Russell Robinson. It is built up of thin bronze laminations riveted to four goatskin leather straps. The upper and largest plate is finished by having its upper edge knocked back and rolled.

Perhaps our last glimpse of a warrior equipped in Sassanian fashion comes from the painted leather surface of a wooden shield found among the debris of the ruined castle of Mug, east of Samarkand, now in Soviet Uzbekistan. A large number of documents were also discovered, enabling experts to date the destruction to the 8th century AD, after the resident noble had rebelled against his Arab overlord. The painting shows a mounted warrior with what is probably either a mace or a fly whisk over his shoulder; his head and legs are missing, but enough of the painting remains to show a long-sleeved coat of what appears to be laminated armour, very similar to a coat of laminates shown among the reliefs of Dacian and Sarmatian arms on the base of Trajan's column in Rome. The horseman's arms are encased in the earliest known representation of the tubular defences known as *basuband*. He carries two unstrung bowstaves in a case on his left hip; arrows are shown at the right hip; a late Sassanid-type sword with a slight curve is slung beneath the bowcase, and he sits an ample horned saddle.

The Sassanid Persian Empire, 5th century AD.

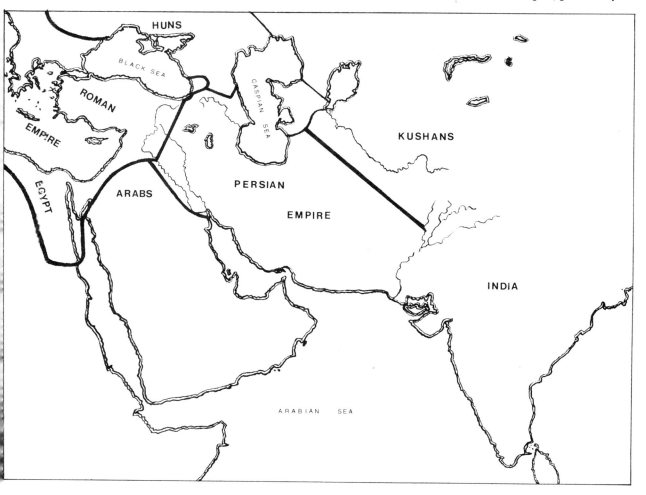

Sassanian Campaigns

The native Persian revival was focused on Fars, a province of southern Iran, where the original nomadic Persian horsemen had settled nearly 1,000 years earlier.

Sassan was a high priest of the temple of Anahita at Persis. His son, Papak, who succeeded to the post, married the daughter of a local prince whom he dislodged in a coup d'etat in AD 208. The Parthian king refused to recognise the seizure, and later would not ratify the succession of Papak's son, Shapur. When Papak died, his second son, Ardashir, who was an officer at Darabgerd in Fars, refused to accept Shapur as king of Persis, and a serious confrontation between the two brothers threatened. The accidental death of Shapur defused the situation, and Ardashir proclaimed himself king, bringing Fars, Isfahan and Kerman under his control and forcing all the petty nobles of the district to recognise him as suzerain. The Parthian king, Artabanus V, ordered the king of Ahwaz to bring this Persian rebel Ardashir to heel. He was quickly defeated; Ardashir then marched against the Parthian army, which he defeated in three successive battles. The last battle was fought in AD 224 at Susiana where the Parthian king, Artabanus, was killed: his head was hung in the temple of Anahita at Persopolis.

Two years later Ardashir was crowned at Ctesiphon, the capital of Parthia. He gave his grandfather's name Sassan to the new Persian dynasty—the 'Sassanids'.

Sassanian sword; the large carrying brackets on the scabbard have staple-like strap attachment loops on the nearer face. The raised medial rib has three embossed curlicues above and below the lower bracket collar; the hilt is spurred to make a recess for the index finger, and has a pommel pierced for a wrist loop. (Trustees of the British Museum)

Chosroes I, the Parthian Arsacid king of Armenia, confronted the new Persian Empire with the dangerous coalition of Armenian, Roman and Scythian forces, together with the army of the Kushans—the king of Kushan had become host to the Parthian royal family. The only noble Parthian clan to join these enemies of the Sassanids were the Karens. Armenia fought for ten years before admitting final defeat. The Scythians and Romans withdrew after severe defeats. The Kushans gradually ceased operations as their troops were bribed to give up their losing fight.

The Sassanid king now turned his attention to the frontiers of his empire, and decided that Rome had to be attacked wherever she impinged on Persian territory. The fortresses of Carrhae and Nisibis were seized and reoccupied by the Persians after intense fighting. When he died in AD 241, Ardashir was able to leave a stable empire defended by a powerful army to his son Shapur, whom he had trained in kingship for several years prior to his death. The late Parthian feudal system was improved by increasing central control.

Shapur's attention was drawn to foreign affairs soon after his accession. The Romans, Kushans, Armenians and Iranian nomads were a constant threat to the frontiers of the new empire. He moved against the Kushans by seizing Peshawar, the Kushan winter capital; occupied the Indus valley; turned north across the Hindu Kush; took Bactria; crossed the Oxus, and rode into Samarkand and Tashkent. The dynasty of Kanishka was deposed, and pro-Persian princes were given a much reduced state of Kushan to govern (AD 241–242).

The Sassanid army had suffered many defeats at the hands of Roman forces in Syria, though they had advanced as far as Antioch. Shapur was preparing a withdrawal back to Iran when Gordianus III, the Roman Emperor, was mur-

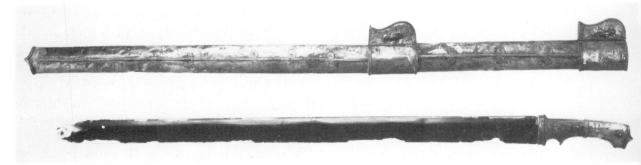

Sassanian chivalry: 'Bas-relief of a king charging an enemy', drawn *in situ* at Taq-i-Bustan (Naqsh-i-Rustem) by Sir Robert Ker-Porter. The relief shows Varham II (AD 276–293) attacking an opponent who has broken his *kontos*. (By permission the British Library; MS Add. 14758)

dered at Zaitha near the Euphrates, probably at the instigation of Philip the Arab, who succeeded him in AD 244. Philip immediately sued for peace: he abandoned Armenia and most of the small principalities, who were still pro-Parthian in Mesopotamia.

War broke out again between Persia and Rome in AD 250, and the Persians took a number of Syrian towns. Antioch was captured by Persian forces in AD 256; Dura Europos was placed under siege and its walls undermined in AD 254. After a great victory near Edessa in AD 260 the Roman Emperor Valerian and 70,000 legionaries were captured by Shapur. The captives were taken to Khuzistan, where they built cities on the lines of a Roman military camp, and settled down with local wives. Eventually they erected a large bridge across the River Karun, where the remains still stand at Shustar. Valerian himself disappeared without trace. Magnificent bas-reliefs carved into the rock cliffs of Fars to celebrate the victories of Shapur show the Emperor Valerian at his feet.

The Persian army took full advantage of its victories, harrying throughout Syria and Cappadocia. During their return march the Palmyrenes made a determined and successful surprise attack on the Persians, capturing huge quantities of booty.

Varham II came to the throne in AD 276, the same year as the Roman Emperor Probus. War was resumed again in Syria, but a peace was quickly negotiated by Varham, who ceded Armenia and Mesopotamia. Thus freed from problems in the west, he was able to deal with his brother, the viceroy of Seistan, who was supported by the prince of Kushan, in an attempt to seize the throne. The resurgent Kushan Empire was destroyed by Shapur II (AD 309–79), and its territory was annexed to the throne as a new province ruled by Sassanian princes from Balkh.

War with Rome in the west to regain the

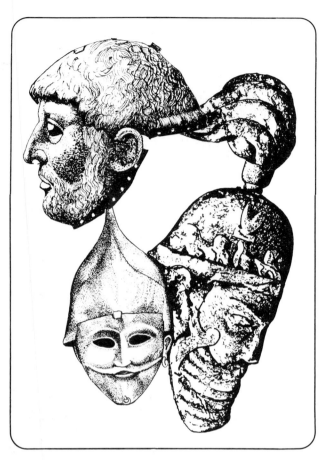

Masked helmets. Lower right: helmeted head of an adversary unseated by Hormizd II; there is a strong possibility that this shows a masked helmet—note angle of skull, lack of brow rim, and what appears to be an embossed pattern on the cheek. Top left: Roman cavalry parade helmet of probable Hellenic manufacture; the bronze skull is treated to represent hair, and there are holes punched along the flanges to take the lacing for a lining. Bottom left: iron helmet of the 10th century from a *kurgan* at Kreis Kanewsk, probably Tartar. With the possible exception of lower right, these examples may give some idea of the Iranian masked helmets mentioned by Heliodorus in the 3rd and by Ammianus Marcellinus in the 4th century AD.

provinces ceded by Varham II and Narsah, a successor, was relentless and protracted. In a battle fought on the River Tigris in AD 363, Persian bowmen lined the bank opposite the Romans to screen the main Persian army who were forming up at some distance behind them. The first line was of heavy, armoured troopers, supported by massed peasant spearmen. The third line was composed of elephants. The Romans made a midnight crossing; dispersing the bowmen lining the bank, they pushed forward to contact the main Persian army, which they reached by mid-morning. The swift Roman advance in battle formation screened by javelineers took the Persians by surprise, minimising

the effect of their storm of arrows. The legions were able to slowly turn the subsequent hand-to-hand fighting into a rout, which developed into a stampede: 2,500 Persians are said to have died for the loss of 75 Romans.

Maranga was fought later the same year. The Persians had their heavy lancers in the centre of the line, with the *clibanarii* on the flanks and elephants to the rear; no infantry seem to have been present. Again, the Romans closed quickly to minimise the effect of the arrow storm; after fairly serious losses the Persian cataphracts made an orderly withdrawal covered by the *clibanarii* bowmen, who shot as they in turn retired. Roman losses were slight.

The same year, AD 363, saw yet another battle at Suma, which began with an attack on the rear of the Roman column under the command of Jovianus by Persian light cavalry; these were driven off by Roman light troops. The column was now subjected to a serious assault led by elephants, who were attacked by two crack legions of the Western armies. Several of the animals were killed, but the dislocation they had caused was exploited by the Persian heavy lancers supported by heavy bowmen. Roman cohesion began to suffer, until troops from another part of the column joined the two legions and drove the Persians off, killing more elephants. They were aided by the baggage train guards, who threw their javelins from a small hill.

The continuing struggle with Rome on the Euphrates was suspended for a time when the eastern territories of Persia were attacked by those Kushans who were still nomads, and by Chionite Ephthalites. The invasion was contained, and the invaders were allocated homelands in Kushan territory, agreeing to furnish auxiliary troops to the Persian army. The Mongoloid Ephthalites eventually became strong enough to expel the Kushans from the territories given them by Persia, and towards the end of the 4th century began an expansion on either side of the Hindu Kush. With the establishment of Christianity as the official religion of Rome and Armenia the enmity between Rome and Persia took on a new intensity, and the increasing power of the aristocratic clans brought to Sassanian Persia the same dynastic upheavals suffered by Arsacid Parthia.

In AD 421 Varham V was involved in a dynastic struggle with his brothers during which he received military aid from the Arabs of Hira, a vassal state in Sassanid Persia. Foreign interference of this kind became a serious threat to the stability of Sassanid Persia, and was one of the causes of its final collapse.

Varham V was evidently a pleasing character, and the most famous of the Sassanian kings. Legends surrounding him speak of his prowess as a poet, a musician, and above all as a hunter; he became a favourite subject for Persian artists for centuries after his death. He was able to neutralise much of the internal strife in his realm by sacrificing many of his prerogatives. He campaigned against the Ephthalites, stabilising and confining their borders. After Varham's death in AD 438, Persia experienced a prolonged drought; the imposition of heavy taxes, together with a disastrous war against the Ephthalites, brought the country near to destruction—King Peroz (AD 459–84) was defeated, taken prisoner, and only released in return for a huge tribute, leaving his son Kavad as a hostage.

Constantinople was interested at this time in a strong Persia, which would help to buffer her eastern provinces from increasing waves of nomads off the steppes. Byzantine policy was one of careful manipulation to produce a stable, but constantly preoccupied buffer state.

During the reign of Peroz the Huns, a Mongoloid people from the Altai, penetrated as far as the provinces of Persia proper, and were evicted only when the imperial army was completely mobilised. Peroz lost his life during a more successful invasion by the Ephthalites soon after the defeat of the Huns. Their success began a century of meddling in Persian affairs. Raids from the northern nomads, especially the Huns, were increasing when the Ephthalites placed Kavad, the son of Peroz, on the Persian throne in AD 488. The situation he faced was one of great internal unrest; the Mazdakite movement was strongly supported by the lower classes in its aims of equalising the distribution of goods (and women—some of the harems belonging to the nobility were unbelievably large). King Kavad championed the movement, introducing laws to 'socialise' the country. His throne was immediately forfeit; he was imprisoned, but managed to escape to take refuge with the Ephthalites in AD 499. They gave him military support, and he recaptured the throne from his brother Zamasp. Tribute was still being paid to the

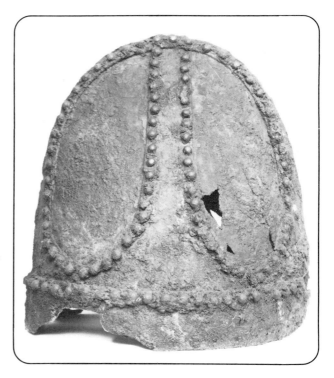

Sassanian helmet of the 4th or 5th centuries AD; a 'spangenhelm' of copper-faced iron, it is in the shape of the traditional Parthian *bashlyk* cap. The headpiece is constructed of four oval plates and a wide headband joined by four narrow plates of inverted 'T'-shape, all secured with ball rivets. Viewed from the front, the helmet appears conical, the sides being brought into the apex in sweeping curves. (Trustees of the British Museum)

Ephthalites, and a bodyguard of their troops was expensively retained. The king's involvement with the Mazdakites ceased when they opposed the nomination of his son Chosroes as heir presumptive.

Kavad died in AD 531, and Chosroes came to the throne at the outset of a trial of strength between the nobles and people. The prince emerged from the long struggle more powerful than any of his predecessors. The army was re-formed, to give each of the four divisions of the empire its own units with a separate commander; compulsory service for peasant soldiers created a militia, as opposed to peasants being conscripted and hastily armed only for a specific campaign. Barbarian tribes were settled on the frontiers as forward defence against nomadic incursion. Forts were built along the Derband pass, and a wall closed the mountain gap south west of the Caspian Sea.

In AD 540 Chosroes refused the usual tribute to the Ephthalites, who were unable to enforce the agreed custom. Two decades later, when the Turks

39

Silver plate, 6th century AD, showing a Sassanian monarch (probably Varham V) destroying a family of lions. (Trustees of the British Museum)

and Persians redrew eastern Persia's borders at the Oxus, the Ephthalites were annihilated.

The new Roman capital, Byzantium, was conscious of growing Persian strength, and set about encircling her great eastern opponent in a noose of potential raiders. In AD 568 trouble broke out in Armenia, and the Persian army fought successfully against the Byzantine army when Roman Mesopotamia was invaded yet again and devastated. Chosroes died during peace negotiations after reigning 50 years. His son, Hormizd (AD 579–90), attempted vainly to maintain the monarch's supremacy over the aristocrats and priesthood, and was soon involved in inter-factional difficulties.

Byzantine diplomacy began to show positive results, and Persia was faced with war on three fronts. Varham Chobin, a great Persian army leader, beat off the Huns in the north and the Turks in the east, but failed against Byzantine troops in the west. Hormizd showed his displeasure with Varham, and the army declared against the king. The great clans seized their hour; King Hormizd was thrown into prison, where he suffered mutilation.

When Chosroes II (AD 590–628), the son of Hormizd, took the throne he was challenged by

40

Varham Chobin; the adventurer took the capital and the throne. Chosroes fled to Byzantium, where the Emperor Maurice gave him troops. Varham was defeated and assassinated, and the throne regained. Maurice was rewarded with nearly all of Armenia and Georgia.

After several years of peace Persian armies moved into Armenia, Edessa and Caesarea, reaching Scutari in AD 610. Persian and Syrian troops took Antioch, Damascus and Jerusalem the following year; 50,000 Christians were massacred, and relics were stolen from the holy city. Gaza was taken in AD 616; the army advanced into Egyptian territory overrunning old Cairo, Alexandria and the Nile valley as far as northern Ethiopia. Turko-Ephthalite advances were rebuffed in the east. Ankara was taken, and Constantinople was placed under siege.

These conquests, unparalleled in Sassanian history, crumbled away when Byzantine counter-conquests liberated Asia Minor and Armenia: Khazar nomads were brought over the Caucasus by the Byzantine Emperor Heraclius. Persia's most important sanctuary at Azerbaijan was seized. In 627 the Byzantines fielded an army of about 70,000 men at Nineveh, where they were met by a demoralised Sassanid army commanded by Razatis. Both armies encamped for the night, and a continuous flow of Sassanian reinforcements arrived till dawn, throughout the engagement and after. The Sassanid army broke camp at dawn and deployed in close order of three columns with crack assault troops, probably *clibanarii*, forming the first two ranks. The whole army faced the rising sun. When the Byzantine army were deployed Razatis

Rock relief of a Sassanian monarch from Taq-i-Bustan, sketched in sepia by Sir Robert Ker-Porter for his manuscripts *Travels in Georgia, Persia, Armenia and Ancient Babylon*, 1821. This study is marred by only one or two minor discrepancies on the shield and quiver harness. The king is armoured as a *clibanarius* of Sassanian heavy cavalry. (By permission the British Library)

challenged Heraclius to single combat. Heraclius accepted, and though wounded himself finally managed to kill Razatis. The Byzantines immediately attacked with the sun at their backs. During the hard-fought battle, which lasted nine hours, the Persians lost 50,000 men, including a high proportion of officers, together with 28 standards. The survivors retired in good order, unharassed by the Byzantines. The Byzantine troops followed the retreat to the new Sassanian capital of Destigerd, which they were able to capture, recovering 300 of their own military standards.

Early in the following spring (AD 628) the Byzantines finally laid siege to Ctesiphon. Chosroes, who had become a sick man, refused to sign the surrender document, and was assassinated by his half-Roman son. The king had been unpopular at his own court: he was surly, cunning, cowardly, suspicious, disloyal, pompous and greedy, and his unceasing demand for troops brought about a nationwide drain on the country's manhood. Persia was also experiencing natural disasters at about this time: the Tigris broke its banks, turning agricultural land into swamps and flooding a large part of Ctesiphon.

Persia fell further into anarchy; the warring factions were ruled over by a dozen kings in 13 years. So many of the male members of the royal house were killed off that the daughters of Chosroes II, Boran and Azarmedukht, had to take the throne. Eventually, the imperial giant began to stagger into a conglomerate of petty states. The new aristocracy created by Chosroes II were not strong enough to prevent the onset of social disintegration, or to resist barbarian invasion from the deserts of Arabia.

In 637 an Islamic army inflicted a crushing defeat on the Sassanians at Qadisiyya; in three days' fighting the Persians were routed, the royal standard was captured, and the commander-in-chief, Rustam, was killed. The final battle against the Islamic tide was fought at Nihawand in 642. The Sassanian peasant infantry are reported to have been chained together to force them to stand their ground. Both Byzantium and Persia had been seriously weakened by the exhausting wars they had fought between 603 and 629; but Persia—shaken by defeat, ruled by an unstable dynasty, her army and civil service disrupted, her people alienated by crushing taxation and parasitic landlords—was the weaker. When the vigorous new impulse of Islam struck them both, it was Persia which collapsed.

Detailed drawing from a photograph of the same carving at Taq-i-Bustan; note the vent in the armour at the horse's throat, allowing free head movement, and the full-face aventail leaving only the eyes exposed.

The Plates

A1, A2: Parthian cataphracts, 1st century BC
The nobleman, A1, has a 'thimble'-shaped bronze helmet with an aventail of iron mail held to the face by a sheathed tie. He has a bronze scale corselet; laminated bronze vambraces protect his arms, and cuisses of bronze scale his legs, the latter suspended from the waist and secured to the legs by straps rather in the manner of the American cowhand's

'chaps'. Their shape is deduced from the rawhide examples from Dura Europos and from a terracotta plaque; although this evidence is of a later period, the essentially similar Scythian examples recovered from much earlier graves attest their use for several centuries. The knight's great sword is slung at a sharp angle below the heavy bronze-faced waist belt. Both men are armed with the long *kontos* lance.

The rider A2 is armoured almost entirely in iron; the thick fabric tabard has laminate shoulder guards and covers a lamellar corselet. His helmet, of 'spangenhelm' construction, has a bronze lamellar aventail. Both horses have three-piece scale armours, one of lacquered rawhide and one of iron, the eyes being protected by deep hemispherical 'baskets' of bronze.

B1: Early Parthian horse-archer, 4th century BC
This ancestral figure is dressed in typical Scythian fashion: a felt *bashlyk*, leather *kaftan*, trousers and short boots, with decorations of appliqué-work and metal plaques. A second, ready-strung bow is carried in the *gorytos*, the combination bowcase and quiver.

B2: Parthian horse-archer, 2nd century BC
This figure is based on the statue of a young noble found in the ruined temple at Shami, Elymais. Settled Parthians seem to have preferred not to cover their carefully arranged hair—when shown as horse-archers they are generally depicted bare-headed. His kaftan of a fine, soft fabric has a felt or leather decorative border; the heavily decorated trousers are protected by thick, tubular fabric 'chaps' slung from the waist.

B3: Parthian horse-archer, 3rd century AD
Based on a terracotta plaque and a wall painting from Dura, this rider has a low, pointed felt cap, a woollen 'pullover' tunic, and patterned trousers again protected by baggy overtrousers. Note the neat leather *gorytos*, a combination case for a spare unstrung bow, arrows, and a short sword in a built-in scabbard.

C1: Parthian cataphract, 2nd century AD
A nobleman, based on the well-known and endlessly argued graffito at Dura. The conical 'spangenhelm', though conjectural, shows the probable appearance of the original attempted in the wall drawing. Some authorities believe that the knight is meant to be wearing a mask, others an open aventail; our interpretation shows a complete aventail hooked up to the helmet rim above the nose, forming a veil-like face defence and leaving two eye vents. The trunk is protected by a coat of combined mail and plates: the top row of plates are attached to the shoulder mail, and the mail skirt is suspended from the lower plates. This form of armour became popular throughout western and central Asia in later centuries.

C2: Armenian cataphract, 3rd century AD
Whenever they took the field with the armies of Iran, Armenian troops held a position of honour. This nobleman has a very Assyrian-looking helmet of early Sassanian pattern. His coat of armour, made up of lamellae laced in counter-reversed rows, is worn over a long-sleeved mail coat, and his legs are protected by mail chausses. This figure represents a probable likeness of the subject suggested by the bas-relief of Goliath at Gagic, Lake Van; though dated to the 11th century, it serves to give some idea of Armenian heavy cavalry armour of earlier times.

His mount is protected by a chamfron, neck guard and peytral, a type of half-armour used by the later Sassanians in their formations of *clibanarii*. The Parthian in the background carries an open-

43

jawed, bronze dragon standard with a tubular silk body; it is suggested that this type of standard, later so widely copied that it was seen in the ranks of late Roman armies and even reached Britain, may have been used by bowmen as a guide to wind speed and direction.

D1: Early Sassanian cataphract, 3rd century AD

The Sassanians' great victory over the Parthian king Artabanus at Susiana in AD 224 is commemorated by the great reliefs of Partho-Sassanian chivalry carved on the rock cliffs at Firusabad. This young squire is based upon the figure of a Sassanian knight pulling a Parthian knight from his mount. He wears a 'thimble'-shaped iron helmet with a bronze motif on either side. The long sleeves of his mail coat reach below his knuckles, a feature clearly shown on the reliefs. A short, fitted tabard of thick fabric is worn over the mail; since the carvings show no folds or creases, some authorities interpret them as breastplates of metal or some other hard substance; but while this is entirely possible, the extreme rarity of such one-piece torso defences throughout western Asia inclines us to the idea of fabric. If we are right, these fabric pieces may well have included built-in protective plates or padding. The horse is armoured in felt, the clan badge being displayed all over the surface, and also on the bow and quiver housings.

D2: Parthian cataphract, 3rd century AD

Based on the figure shown wrestling with the young Sassanian D1 in the rock carvings, he wears a plumed iron helmet with a scale aventail. The sleeveless coat of bronze lamellae is covered to the waist by a thick fabric tabard; the limbs are protected by iron laminate defences. The horse is unarmoured, as were many Partho-Sassanian heavy cavalry mounts. Two large tassels hang from the breast strap, and metal ornaments adorn the rump; the tail is hung with pleated fabric streamers.

D3: Sassanian standard-bearer

This is the standard of Fars, representing the sun orb, moon and wings of Ahuramazda; we show the bearer as a mounted noble, but it could equally have been carried by a lowlier infantry officer. He wears a 'spangenhelm' helmet of Assyrian appearance, a long-sleeved mail shirt, and baggy trousers over leg defences of laminates or mail.

E1: Sassanian clibanarius, 6th century AD

Based upon the figures of two warriors in combat engraved on a silver plate, both of whom wear a peculiar kind of helmet: basically conical, it has a secondary point on either side of the shell and a small globe at the apex. We must here admit defeat: the helmet construction is not understood, and we substitute for it here a known Sassanian style. The coat of bi-lobed lamellae covers a shorter, long-sleeved mail coat, and the legs and feet are protected by laminated armour. In earlier times heavy cavalrymen of this class were not equipped with shields, but they were evidently introduced by the 6th century. Half-armour for horses became more popular in the later Sassanian period.

E2: Sassanian war elephant

A hypothetical reconstruction based on several relevant sources, including ancient representations. The Indian elephant bears a crenelated wooden *howdah* holding two mercenary bowmen; the *mahout* is Indian. The tusks are sheathed with bronze. Despite their unpredictability on the battlefield, the fact that war elephants were used throughout ancient and Oriental medieval history right up until the widespread introduction of gunpowder would seem to argue for some degree of success—although tradition probably also played a part in their retention.

F1: Nomadic Iranian horse-archer

These troops were raised by the Sassanians from the nomadic and semi-nomadic tribes on the north-eastern borders of their empire. They were subject or allied peoples, related to the Parthians. The ponies' manes were cut in many different patterns: we are reminded of the 13th-century Mongols, who had a whole system of cuts related to age and sex.

F2: Chionite-Ephthalite horse-archer

A Mongoloid nomad people, related to the Hunnish tribes which followed the westerly migration of Caucasoid Iranian tribes such as the Scytho-Sarmatians off the steppes and into western Asia and eastern Europe. He is equipped in the same way as the Iranian horse-archer, though with a larger composite bow, and carries a lariat.

F3: Nomadic standard-bearer

Nomads were given to using horse or yak tails as standards; and as with the dragon standard, they may have been useful as guides to wind speed and direction for the predominantly bow-armed riders. This man is from one of the Iranian tribes which

The conquests of Islam in western Asia: broken lines indicate conquests under Mohammed, 622–632; dotted shading indicates conquests under the caliphs, 632–661; and circles indicate conquests under the Umayyads, 661–750. See also MAA 125, *The Armies of Islam 7th–11th Centuries*.

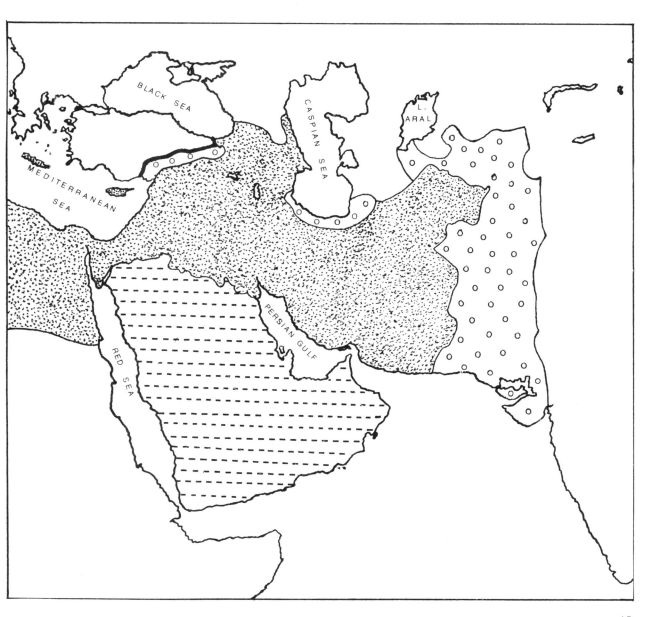

drifted about the great Eurasian plains; he would lead a division of mounted archers, acting as a rallying-point in battle. His corselet is made of split and polished horn or hoof, mounted in close-set rows of scales on a fabric jerkin; tunic and trousers are of wool, and boots of soft leather. The stricken Roman is a member of one of the new élite Auxilia Palatina units raised by Constantine in the 4th century.

G1: Sassanian levy spearman

These peasant levies from the countryside of Iran were forced into military service at need; hardly trained, they were used as general duties personnel and baggage guards as well as acting as a spear phalanx in battle. Their indifferent quality is

The blazon from the remains of a round, leather-covered wooden shield found in the ruins of the stronghold of Mug in Ferghana, which was destroyed in the 8th century AD. The painting shows a horseman wearing laminated armour, and what may be the earliest representation of the arm defences of plate known as *basuband*. (Hermitage Museum, Leningrad)

indicated by the fact that they were chained together by the ankles on the field of Nihawand in 642. This spearman has a leather-covered cane shield, a simple spear and a short sword.

G2: Syrian foot-archer

A mercenary from northern Syria, he is armed with a large composite bow, an axe and a bullhide shield. He wears a felt cap and a woollen tunic and trousers.

G3: Anatolian slinger

The tough hillmen of western Asia were hired by eastern Romans, Sassanians and Byzantines alike. This highlander carries a small target shield, to knock aside missiles or blows, and carries his stones in a goatskin bag. Hard to detect in flight, and difficult to dodge, sling pellets could stun, maim or even kill, and were extremely dangerous even to armoured troops.

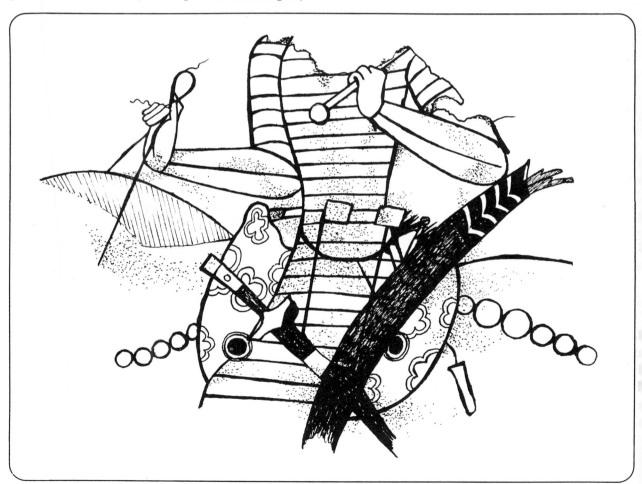

G4: Kurdish javelineer

Typical costume of woollen tunic and trousers and short boots is supplemented by a sheepskin jerkin; the target is of stained hide. These hillmen used javelin-thongs to increase the power of the throw and to spin the missile in flight, for accuracy.

G5: Sassanian cataphract, 5th century AD

Some Sassanian heavy cavalry units were equipped in the Parthian tradition, completely armoured, man and horse. They were not bowmen, but were armed with the *kontos*, long sword, and a mace or axe. Their masked helmets must have limited visibility and thus agility in battle. Their reliance for support upon lighter troopers in the ranks of the *clibanarii* was occasionally misplaced; this may be the reason that these units were later discontinued.

H1: Sassanian clibanarius, 7th century AD

This rider is based on what is probably the best-known high-relief carving of an Iranian heavy cavalryman, mounted on a powerful half-armoured horse. The head, neck and chest defences are made of rows of close-set, overlapping curved-sided lamellae attached to a tough fabric backing. The resemblance between this helmet—taken, like the rest of this figure, from the fully-armoured king carved into the rock at Taq-i-Bustan near Kermanshah—and those recovered from Scandinavian graves at Vendel and Valsgarde in Sweden is remarkable. The mail aventail, like Byzantine examples, may have been of triple thickness. The long-sleeved mail coat is supplemented by hand guards and a small round shield; his legs are probably armoured under the long skirt. The Taq-i-Bustan carving shows the decorations proper to a monarch.

H2: Sassanian standard-bearer

The standard, with five pomegranate symbols and fabric streamers, must have been difficult to handle on horseback: we may guess that it would often have been carried by a dismounted nobleman. The Parthian-shaped helmet bears a motif on either side of the skull which may have been an identification device; it has leather neck and cheek guards.

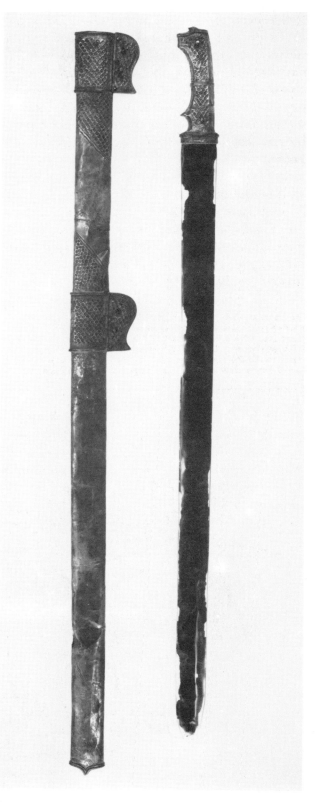

Sassanian sword; once more, the 'honeycomb' pattern on areas of the scabbard is continued up on to the hilt and the bulky collars and brackets of this handsome weapon, and the pommel is pierced for a wrist loop. (Trustees of the British Museum)

Plates Sources

The sources for the plates are too numerous to list separately for each figure. Some of the plates are conjectural, others less so—there are yawning gaps in our knowledge of Partho-Sassanian military fashion, the sophistication of which set the pattern for the arming of Asia and influenced the chivalry of Europe. All these figures are based upon rock carvings, statues, wall paintings, graffiti, silver platters, goblets, rhytons, coins, and archaeological finds in western Asia; Greek and Roman armour, bas-reliefs, statues and contemporary written accounts of late Roman and Asian heavy cavalry. The opinions of respected authorities on western Asian military technology have been consulted and used where relevant; and recourse has been made to material from other periods of Asian and European history, for useful comparisons in matters of construction and use of armour.

Notes sur les planches en couleur

A1 L'armure de jambe est une reconstitution d'après des objets d'une époque précédente trouvés dans des tombes scythiques et des exemples ultérieurs en cuir provenant de Dura Europos. **A2** L'armure de torse en tissu épais possède des pièces d'épaule lamellées et couvre un corselet d'armure lamellé. Les deux chevaux ont des caparaçons d'armure fabriqués en trois éléments, un en cuir laqué et l'autre en écailles de fer. Les deux cavaliers portent la lance "kontos".

B1 Vêtements scythiques caractéristiques, en laine, feutre et cuir, décorés de pièces appliquées et de plaques de métal. Un arc de réserve est porté, déjà tendu, dans le carquois/étui à arc combinés. **B2** Basé sur une statue de Shami, Elymaïs; noter la coiffure soigneusement arrangée et sur-pantalon tubulaire accroché à la taille comme des "chaps" de cow-boy. **B3** Basé sur une peinture murale de Dura Europos; noter le sur-pantalon large et l'étui d'arc/carquois/fourreau d'épée habilement combinés.

C1 D'après le graffito le plus célèbre de Dura Europos; les avis diffèrent, mais nous voyons ici un petit voile de mailles sur le visage accroché au casque. L'armure de corps de mailles et de plaques combinées est d'une forme qui devint populaire en Asie occidentale dans les siècles ultérieurs. **C2** Le casque de style assyrien du type de la fin de l'époque sassanide est porté avec une armure lamellée de torse sur une cotte de mailles et des protections de membres en mailles. Le cheval porte une demi armure, ce qui est un style commun à la fin de l'époque sassanide. L'étendard "draco" qui devint de plus en plus populaire à la fin de l'Empire romain et se répandit jusqu'en Grande Bretagne peut avoir eu une valeur pratique, indiquant la vitesse et la direction du vent aux archers.

D1 D'après les célèbres sculptures de Firusabad, montrant la victoire sassanide sur les Parthes à Susiana, an 224. Les autorités ne sont pas d'accord sur le torse; il est lisse et sans plis et certaines autorités disent qu'il s'agit d'une cuirasse; mais une telle armure est très rare en Asie et il est plus probable qu'il s'agisse d'un tissu. L'armure en feutre du cheval porte l'insigne du clan. **D2** Sur la base de la même sculpture d'un cavalier sassanide faisant tomber un Parthe de la selle—voir dessin du texte principal. De nombreux chevaux de cavalerie ne portaient pas d'armure. **D3** Etendard de Fars, montrant le soleil, la lune et les ailes d'Ahuramazda. Les pantalons larges sont portés sur une armure de bandes lamelées ou de mailles.

E1 A cette date, des boucliers commençaient à apparaître. Noter l'armure de membres. Une demi-armure pour les chevaux devint plus commune à la fin de la période sassanide. **E2** Reconstruction conjecturale basée sur des sources anciennes; l'éléphant et son mahout sont indiens, les archers sont des mercenaires.

F1 Recrutés parmi les tribus nomades soumises des frontières nord-est de l'empire iranien qui étaient du même sang que les Parthes. La crinière des chevaux était coupée selon plusieurs styles différents. **F2** Les nomades mongoliques de cette tribu créèrent d'innombrables difficultés pour les monarques sassanides et dominèrent l'Iran pendant plusieurs périodes. **F3** L'armure de torse est en corne ou sabot fendu et poli.

G1 Ces troupes étaient composées de paysans aux armes simples et à la formation très insuffisante étaient si peu fiables qu'à la bataille de Nihawand ces soldats étaient enchaînés les uns aux autres pour les empêcher de fuir. **G2** Mercenaire bien entraîné du nord de la Syrie, armé d'un grand arc de construction mixte, d'un bouclier en cuir et d'un coup-de-poing. **G3** Toutes les puissances de l'Asie occidentale employaient ces durs montagnards. La pierre de fronde était difficile à voir et à éviter; elle pouvait blesser ou tuer même des hommes portant l'armure. **G4** La lanière enroulée autour du javelin le faisait tourner pendant le vol, lui donnant une précision plus grande. **G5** Certaines unités sassanides de cavalerie lourde étaient équipées dans l'ancien style des Parthes, avec des casques masqués; ces casques étaient très beaux mais ils devaient limiter dangereusement le champ de vision.

H1 Basé sur une sculpture d'un roi sassanide à Taq-i-Bustan. La similarité entre ce casque et des exemples suédois à peu près contemporains trouvés à Vendel et Valsgarde est extraordinaire. **H2** Le casque, de forme parthe, a un motif qui est peut-être un moyen d'identification sur les côtés ainsi que des rabats de joues et de cou en cuir.

Farbtafeln

A1 Der Beinschutz ist nach frühen skythischen Grabfunden und späteren ledernen Teilen aus Dura Europos rekonstruiert. **A2** Der Torso-Panzer aus dickenm Stoff hat beschichtete Schulterstücke und bedeckt einen Plattenpanzerharnisch. Beide Pferde haben ein dreiteiliges, gepanzertes Geschirr, eines mit lackiertem Leder, das andere mit Eisenplatten. Die Reiter tragen Kontos-Lanzen.

B1 Typische Skytherbekleidung aus Wolle, Filz und Leder, verziert mit Applikationen und Metallplatten. Ein bereits gespannter Ersatzbogen wird im kombinierten Pfeil/Bogenköcher mitgeführt. **B2** Nach einer Statue aus Shami in Elymaïs; man beachte das sorgfältig gelegte Haar und die röhrenförmigen Überhosen, wie Cowboy-Chaps um die Hüften geschlagen. **B3** Nach einer Wandmalerei aus Dura Europos; man beachte die weiten Überhosen und die Kombination von Bogen/Pfeilköcher und Schwertscheide.

C1 Nach den bekanntesten Wandzeichnungen in Dura Europos; es gibt verschiedene Interpretationen, aber wir halten das Gesicht für die Darstellung eines Kettenschleiers, der am Helm aufgehängt wird. Diese Form des Körperpanzers, eine Kombination aus Ketten und Platten, wurde in späteren Jahrhunderten in Westasien populär. **C2** Der im assyrischen Stil gehaltene Helm vom späten sassanischen Typ wird mit Torso-Plattenpanzer über einem Kettenhemd und Kettenschutz für die Gliedmassen getragen. Das Pferd ist zur Hälfte gepanzert, ein typischer spätsassonischer Brauch. Die Drako-Standarte, die im ganzen spätrömischen Weltreich bis hinauf nach Britannien verbreitet war, hatte möglicherweise auch eine praktische Bestimmung und gab den Bogenschützen Informationen über Windrichtung und -stärke.

D1 Nach den berühmten Schnitzereien von Firusabad; ein sassanidischer Sieg über die Parther bei Susiana (224 n.Chr.). Die Fachwelt streitet sich über den Torso; er ist glatt und ohne Falten geschnitzt und stellt nach Ansicht einiger Gelehrter einen Brustpanzer dar, aber ein solcher Panzer ist in Asien ausgesprochen selten, und Stoff ist ein naheliegenderes Material. Die Filzpanzerung für das Pferd trägt das Sippenzeichen. **D2** Nach der gleichen Schnitzerei; ein sassanischer Krieger ringt einen Parther aus dem Sattel (vgl. Zeichnung im Textteil). Viele Kavalleriepferde waren ungepanzert. **D3** Die Standarte von Fars mit der Sonne, dem Mond und den Flügeln von Ahuramazda. Die weiten Hosen werden über Beinpanzern aus beschichteten Streifen oder Ketten getragen.

E1 Zu diesem Zeitpunkt wurden die ersten Schilde eingeführt. Man beachte die Panzerung der Gliedmassen. Halbpanzerung für Pferde wurde in der spätsassonischen Periode populärer. **E2** Spekulative Rekonstruktion nach antiken Quellen; der Elefant und sein Mahout stammen aus Indien, die Bogenschützen sind Söldner.

F1 Diese aus den nomadischen Stämmen der nordöstlichen Grenzen des iranischen Reiches bezogenen Völker waren mit den Parthern verwandt. Die Pferdemähne konnte auf verschiedene Weise geschnitten werden. **F2** Mongoloide Nomaden dieses Stammes bereiteten den sassonischen Herrschern endlose Probleme und beherrschten den Iran für lange Perioden. **F3** Der Torsopanzer ist aus poliertem Hufhorn.

G1 Diese einfach bewaffneten und unzureichend ausgebildeten Bauernsoldaten waren so unzuverlässig, dass sie während der Schlacht von Nihawand an den Fussgelenken zusammengekettet wurden, damit sie nicht fliehen konnten. **G2** Ein geschickter Söldner aus Nordsyrien, mit einem grossen Bogen aus gemischtem Material, einem Schild aus Stierhaut und einer Handaxt bewaffnet. **G3** Alle Reiche in Westasien stellten diese kräftigen Hochländer ein. Die Steinschleuder war kaum zu sehen und schwer zu vermeiden, sie konnte selbst bewaffnete Männer lähmen und töten. **G4** Die um den Wurfspeer gewundene Schnur ermöglicht es, diese Waffe mit grösserer Genauigkeit anzupeilen. **G5** Einige sassanische schwerbewaffnete Kavallerie-Einheiten waren im alten parthischen Stil ausgerüstet, mit Maskenhelmen, die sehr eindrucksvoll aussahen, aber wohl ein begrenztes Sichtfeld gaben.

H1 Nach der Schnitzerei eines sassanischen Königs in Taq-i-Bustan. Die Ähnlichkeit zwischen diesem Helm und weitgehend gleichzeitigen schwedischen Exemplaren aus Vendel und Valsgarde ist ausserordentlich gross. **H2** Der Helm mit der parthischen Form hat wahrscheinlich zur Identifizierung dienende Stücke zu beiden Seiten und lederne Hals- und Wangenklappen.